"CALLING HELLER I THE ENCYCLOPEDI... NANCE."

"WE MADE OUR ESTIMATE (OF THE S&L BAIL-OUT COST) WITH THE HELP OF ECONOMIST WARREN HELLER OF *VERIBANC*."

Warren Heller gives you the crucial financial information you can bank on . . .

- Causes of the current bank and S&L crisis and its extent

- Current trends and possible futures

- What happens when a bank or S&L fails

- What to do if your bank or S&L fails

- Problems you can have if you owe the bank money

- Three specific tests which have predicted over 95 percent of all bank and S&L failures

- How your bank may really be an S&L in disguise

- Common characteristics that strong banks share

- The new rules and dynamics of real estate

- Career opportunities

- AND MUCH MORE!

IS YOUR MONEY SAFE?

HOW TO PROTECT YOUR SAVINGS IN THE CURRENT BANKING CRISIS

WARREN G. HELLER

BERKLEY BOOKS, NEW YORK

IS YOUR MONEY SAFE?

A Berkley Book / published by arrangement with
the author

PRINTING HISTORY
Berkley edition / June 1990

ISBN: 0-425-12496-7

TABLE OF CONTENTS

This book is a guide to help you learn how to protect your money. Since the financial health of any organization can change rapidly, it is important that you carefully investigate any institution in which you plan to invest your money. While the author has tried to include accurate and up-to-date information, neither he nor the publisher will be responsible for inaccuracies or for changes in economic conditions that may affect your investments.

ACKNOWLEDGMENTS

Quite a team of people contributed to this work. My wife, my management and VERIBANC's president (all one person) served as my mentor and made the project possible. The company's staff also provided considerable help, especially Dr. Lawreen Connors, who reviewed early draft copy. The efforts of outside reviewers—Elizabeth Watts, Literary Consultant; Trish Todd of Berkley Publishing; Dr. Hugh McLaughlin, Professor of Finance (Bentley College) and Don Inscoe of the FDIC—are all gratefully appreciated. Of course, if there are any problems, the buck stops here.

—Warren G. Heller

The unsung heroes of the banking crisis are the people at FDIC, OCC, FRB, OTS (as well as FHLBB before it) and the NCUA who kept this country's financial system together for the past decade. Often at great sacrifice to their personal and family lives and, in some cases, their careers, thousands of people in these agencies have accomplished what would rightfully have been considered an impossible task. No one, in 1975, could have conceived that we could stand the failures of hundreds of institutions per year and a financial drain of more than one third of a trillion dollars without also suffering a major financial collapse.

Their accomplishments have been all the more remarkable in view of the barrage of roadblocks put up by elements in Congress, the various administrations and the different industry lobbies. Although they were not always right (and this book takes issue with several of their policies), the bottom line is that they have been right enough, often enough, to hold the system together and maintain the reign of prosperity. History should well remember with gratitude the teams led by the likes of William Isaac, William Seidman, Robert Clarke, Edwin Gray, Richard Pratt, Todd Conover and Danny Wall. This book is dedicated to them and their accomplishments.

IS YOUR MONEY SAFE?

HOW TO PROTECT YOUR SAVINGS IN THE CURRENT BANKING CRISIS

INTRODUCTION

- One bank in sixty-six now fails each year.
- Over forty billion dollars is owed to our major banks by so-called third world and less developed countries.
- This amount could buy the current "Star Wars" anti-missile defense program or NASA's space station with billions left over.
- Over one-fifth of all savings and loan associations are insolvent (but many still operate, because the government cannot afford to close them).
- It will take over $300 billion (the S&L bailout) for the government to make good on its pledge that insured savings and loan associations' depositors will not lose their money.
- The costs of the bailout could buy living quarters for every homeless person in the country.
- If the S&L bailout money were to be raised in one year, it would divert three thousand dollars from every income tax return filed.

The current turmoil in the banking industry, the conditions that spawned it, and the government policies that both dampen and aggravate the problems, have created a climate in which thousands of banks, savings and loan associations and credit unions are struggling to survive. Banking in the 1990s has become a rough and tumble world, as banks and their creditors, depositors, borrowers and investors have to confront a whole new issue—*bank safety*. Compounding the problem is the fact that vast quantities of money are needed to resolve the crisis. Government agencies, financial institutions seeking to remain solvent and their employees at all levels are caught in crises, mostly not of their making. In response, they are creating a host of products, policies, practices and problems, some of which will separate banking consumers from funds they currently think are safe. Some of the dangers in today's banking world are as subtle as the fine print in a mortgage contract; some are as obvious as a Closed sign on an S&L's front door. However, all need to be understood by anyone who deals with U.S. banking institutions during the final decade of the twentieth century.

The chapters that follow describe the risks customers face at most banking institutions. We give examples of unpleasant surprises that have recently befallen depositors, borrowers and investors, small and large. We offer advice on how to sidestep traps being generated by the ongoing banking crisis. We also provide road maps that can be used to find financial institutions that are safe, and to avoid those that are not. The names of some of the most conservatively run banks in the country are also included.

Throughout this book, the word bank is often used in its broadest possible sense—to connote commercial banks, savings banks, savings and loan associations and credit unions. This helps avoid the cumbersomeness of naming each kind of institution. We apologize to those purists who find distasteful this expediency of calling all banking-type institutions by the more simple, popular name, "banks."

1

BIRTH OF A BANKING CRISIS

The Banking Business

Banking is a very simple business. A bank borrows money from its depositors at low interest rates and, in turn, lends that same money at higher interest rates. It keeps the difference, called "spread" in industry jargon, to pay for its cost of doing business. Part of the spread also goes into profit or "return," although certain kinds of banking institutions do not call it that.

Many banks have branched out into other businesses associated with the borrowing and lending of money. It is not uncommon for today's banks to simplify the payment of bills for customers (through checking or NOW accounts), guarantee promises of payment in business transactions, manage people's financial affairs for them and provide trust administration services.

Although the fees associated with these additional services are often lucrative, the business of banking is principally borrowing and lending. A bank must be sure, when it makes a loan, that the money will be repaid. It must also convince depositors that their money is safe, can be drawn upon when desired, and will be returned at the end of an agreed upon period. Occasionally bankers forget these fundamentals, to their chagrin. In fact, the ongoing banking and S&L crises in the United States have grown out of inadequate attention by bankers and their government regulators to these banking basics. Comptroller of the Currency Robert L. Clarke put it well with his statement, "Banks don't fail. Bankers do."

Why Banks Tend to Be Unstable

When noted bank robber Willie Sutton was asked why he held up banks, he answered, "That is where the money is." Sutton knew what some of today's bankers may have forgotten—banks are essentially unstable institutions because they contain large amounts of money.

Banks have always been the prey of choice for adventurers, desperadoes, revolutionaries and holdup men. Banks are also vulnerable to governments, which exact their toll with more legitimacy (usually!) through taxes, regulation or outright takeover. In either case, there is the danger of demands outstripping an institution's ability to meet them, causing it to go under and its depositors and other creditors to suffer.

Changeable business conditions are another source of instability. Borrowers may be in good financial shape when they take out a loan, but events can turn against them and leave them unable to repay. Many people overextend themselves or their organizations by taking on too much debt. Of course, part of a banker's job is to prevent loan customers from overloading themselves, but often bankers miss the telltale signs of overextension. A borrower's finances may be especially complex; the borrower may provide fraudulent data or the banker may be overconfident about the borrower's financial strength. In bad economic times whole classes of borrowers may default, creating such large losses at the banks that they fail too. This is what happened in Texas during the late 1980s.

Depositors' fear is the source of instability that most

4

worries bankers. Many good banks have failed simply because of an unfounded rumor. Upon hearing the rumor, depositors "run" to the bank and demand their money. (Hence the term "bank run.") Since most of any well-managed bank's money is lent out, little is available for more than the customary pace of withdrawals. Needless to say, when people are told by the bank that they cannot have their money, fear turns into panic, the word spreads rapidly and most of the bank's depositors seek immediate return of their funds. In the past, if a bank possessed insufficient reserves, was unable to "call in" loans rapidly enough or raise enough money to stop a run quickly (by paying depositors), it failed. The irony of this situation, of course, is that if a run is set off by a silly or false rumor, the bank could still be unable to meet the demands of its depositors. In such a case, both bank and depositors alike become victims of a self-fulfilling prophecy. For this reason, runs are one of a banker's greatest fears.

Modern Stabilizers

Two aspects of modern banking in the United States help diminish, but do not eliminate, the danger of runs on banks. The first is the existence of several mechanisms used for near-instantaneous borrowing among banks. Almost any bank that is in good financial condition can draw upon other banks for money to tide it over temporary requirements, such as unusual account withdrawal activity. (In fact, even banks in difficulty can often draw funds from other banks.) If cash is needed, in most instances, it can be obtained in the time it takes for a crosstown trip by an armored truck.

The second stabilizer is the well-known federal deposit insurance that provides complete coverage for depositors whose total account holdings at a bank are $100,000 or

5

less. While the insurance helps prevent runs by small depositors, current regulatory thinking is that it has been too successful in this regard, that most people in the country are too complacent about their bank dealings, regardless of the problems their institution may be having. For this reason, federal deposit insurance reform, which will involve passing along some of the risk of bank failure to account holders (but not enough to cause runs, so the thinking goes), will receive considerable government attention in the 1990s. Government regulators want the small depositor to be more careful about the condition of his or her bank.

How the Current Banking Crisis Was Born

During the last decade, over one thousand banks failed during what were relatively prosperous times. If S&L and credit union failures are included, the number is much higher. Exceptions to this prosperity included portions of the agricultural, energy and real estate sectors of the economy. The S&L industry sank into such a sorry state that Federal regulators let hundreds of insolvent institutions continue to operate, because they did not possess the funds to close them and pay off the insured depositors. In addition to these failures, many of the nation's largest banks teetered on the edge of insolvency because of heavy lending to third world countries that threatened to default on their loans. The present banking crisis is really a collection of many crises, each affecting different parts of the banking industry. The causes of these crises are described below.

Risk Management. During the 1960s and 1970s, sophisticated bankers developed a strange concept. Their idea was that a certain amount of exceedingly risky debt was okay. These bankers reasoned that if a sufficiently higher interest rate was charged on loans that were likely to default, then the losses from the problem loans would average out with the additional interest collected from those risky loans that were repaid. The good borrower would, in effect, pay for the loans that went bad. Risk management bankers assumed that they could accurately measure a borrower's ability to repay. As it turned out, proper assessment of repayment chances must take into account the way in which the entire world economy will affect creditors, whether they be oil businessmen, real estate magnates or entire nations. Hindsight shows that risk management bankers were mistaken in thinking they could so finely calibrate the creditworthiness of their borrowers.

The S&L Problems. Savings and loan associations, or S&Ls, are banking institutions that were given special status and tax breaks by the government in 1934. The purpose of this arrangement was to make home purchase financing readily available to consumers. For years the S&Ls operated smoothly following the so-called 3-6-3 rule: Pay depositors 3 percent and lend money at 6 percent. The final three refers to both the amount of ''spread'' enjoyed by the institution and the time of the afternoon by which the S&L banker was to be on the golf course.

This arrangement went awry in the 1970s when inflation forced S&Ls to pay depositors interest rates over 10 percent. With most of their funds locked into mortgages that were earning 6 or 7 percent, many S&Ls faced negative spreads and began losing money rapidly. To ''help them,'' Congress passed legislation (the Garn St. Germain Depository Institutions Act of 1982) that allowed S&Ls to expand into areas of finance traditionally reserved for banks. By now the distinction between S&Ls and banks has become so blurred that, from a consumer's perspective, the main difference is in the source of their federal deposit insurance. (More details in Chapter 2.) In summary, the present disaster is the result of the way S&Ls raised money; the inflation of the 1970s; and misguided

7

efforts by the industry, the regulators and Congress to correct matters in the early 1980s. The damage to the S&L industry has only begun to be tallied. Here is the score:

- A recently passed bailout law (The Financial Institutions Reform, Recovery and Enforcement Act, FIRREA, enacted August 9, 1989) severely limits business operations at many S&Ls.
- Over $100 billion of government funds are spent on or committed to the S&L bailout.
- Over eight hundred insolvent or near-insolvent S&Ls are under direct government control, are about to be taken over or may be allowed to remain independent as long as they are too costly to close.
- Fewer than half of the remaining two thousand S&Ls can be considered financially healthy.
- Total bailout costs to U.S. taxpayers are conservatively estimated to be close to $300 billion, or about $1,000 per person in the country. (Our studies at VERIBANC indicate that the debacle could easily become even more expensive.)

As of this writing, S&Ls continue to lose $19 billion per year. During 1989 alone, losses accelerated in every quarter. In the final part of the year, thrifts lost over $90 million dollars per day. The bureaucracy created by the 1989 bailout law appears to be paralyzed and is unable to dispose of the wreckage of the failed institutions. Even the solvent S&Ls are threatened by a hostile Congress and exacting regulators. Several observers believe that, within a few years, most remaining S&Ls will either go under or be absorbed into banks, leaving a sharply diminished industry.

Overseas Lending Problems at U.S. Banks. Like the S&L crisis, the trend toward excessive lending to third world countries with an inability to repay was a product of the 1970s. As bankers reached to new borrowers beyond U.S. borders, they were dazzled by the interest rates they could charge and by the literally royal treatment they received from their host countries. Projects the banks financed promised to bring many less developed regions into the modern era. In the heady 1970s the leaders of the nation's largest banks thought they were doing very well by doing good.

These bankers came back to earth after many countries ran into difficulties following price drops in the commodities they sold overseas. Then, in 1982, Mexico announced it was stopping its repayments to U.S. banks. At that time, U.S. banks had some $320 billion of overseas lending, with $98.6 billion out to third world countries. Banks and their government regulators refused to publicly acknowledge that a significant problem existed, despite the fact that private sector analysts and news media routinely developed and printed lists of banks that could be seriously affected by nonpayment of overseas loans. As U.S. banks now flee the third world, their lending to those less developed countries (or LDCs) stands at $42.6 billion (year end 1989).

Tense negotiations between the banks and the individual debtor countries continued throughout the 1980s, and so far, no major defaults have occurred. (Mexico later resumed its payments.) Several countries, most notably Argentina and Brazil, are currently delinquent but so far have not repudiated their obligations. Unlike the S&Ls, the banks can earn their way out of their excessive third world loan exposure. Since profits at the large banks that hold these loans ordinarily run about $15 billion per year, they can make progress toward recovery by acknowledging partial losses on the worst of the debt from time to time. In fact, a few large banks have already given up completely on their third world loans (Morgan Guaranty, for example). Overseas debt could, in a few years, be reduced to the point where it is no longer a significant threat for most banks, provided no major defaults or serious new problems develop.

Phase One of the Real Estate Crash. Overbuilding of office space and, to a lesser extent, residential projects, was fueled by strong demand for real estate in the early 1980s. Inflation also toyed with developers' judgment. Many projects that "did not quite make economic sense" at the time they were started were begun anyway in the expectation that lease and sale prices would continue to rise during the course of construction. Once started, of course, real estate building projects must be pushed on to completion or most of the monies invested are lost. Texas and the Southwest were affected most severely. From the mid-1980s, banks as well as S&Ls in that region suffered serious losses. Many were closed as a result. At the low point in Oklahoma in 1988, a bumper sticker was seen to proclaim "Live Dangerously, Bank in Oklahoma!"

The Agricultural Dimension to Real Estate Problems. The multi-year drought, which caused considerable economic difficulty in the farm belt states, also affected real estate. Many farmers had borrowed heavily to buy land during the 1970s inflation. When farm surplus gluts drove food prices down and the subsequent drought cut farmers' ability to produce, thousands of farmers defaulted on their land loans and home mortgages. Conditions grew rougher than many had imagined. Unrest erupted. Bankers were shot. Gun battles and armed standoffs occurred as those with "nothing left to lose" directed their anger and frustration at the people or institutions they believed to be responsible for their plight. This violence was generally played down by the media. New ghost towns formed in the midwest and plains states, and hundreds of banks failed when unsalable, repossessed real estate was piled on top of their already overwhelming burdens of defaulted agricultural loans.

Phase Two of the Real Estate Crash. After the drought ended in 1988, economic conditions worsened in the

Northeast, along the Atlantic seaboard, in Florida and throughout parts of California. As high-technology investment slowed, and resistance to high prices grew, real estate demand in those areas began to decline. Tighter income tax laws also made investors more reluctant to take on unprofitable property in the hope that tax benefits and later earnings would make up for early losses. Bankers, assuming that prices and demand for property would continue to increase, had kept loan standards easy. Problems followed that continue to unfold today.

Junk Bonds. With the well-publicized troubles of several large issuers of "securities below investment grade," and the demise of Drexel Burnham Lambert, the leading junk bond securities firm, the market for junk bonds is in a turmoil. As of this writing, failures of other institutions specializing in "high yield securities" appear imminent. In addition, S&Ls are required by the 1989 Thrift Bailout Law to unload their $13.5 billion of "junk holdings" by year end 1992, a step sure to depress the market further. However, it is still too soon to assert that a junk bond-driven banking crisis is occurring. That could change, of course, if an economic weakening causes many more companies to default on their high interest rate obligations and loans they have taken to support highly leveraged transactions (takeovers and the like).

Dishonesty and Incompetence. Much press has been given to the criminal elements that have used bank or S&L charters as licenses for fraud, self-dealing and abuse. While the public has recently witnessed the prosecution of many bankers and the chronicling of graft to U.S. House and Senate members, financial institutions have always been a target for this type of insider crime. Although criminal activity has certainly contributed to the banking crisis, especially in the S&L industry, skullduggery has become a convenient target for legislators and regulators who would rather point to shenanigans than accept responsibility for their own, far larger share of the costs. Many bankers and S&L managers simply responded to events outside of their control; their incompetence and inexperience is more to blame than their dishonesty. They now are being vilified by the same political leaders who ignored the problem as it developed from the policies those leaders created. Unfortunately, a number of new, equally self-defeating policies are now being developed.

The Role of Credit Unions

Credit unions are institutions that typically offer personal banking services such as savings accounts (called share accounts—a name that fosters the image of membership by account holders) and personal loans. Credit unions are most frequently run by large employers, unions, trade associations or common-interest groups who operate them as nonprofit institutions, often subsidizing their facilities. They are usually quite small and are managed by a staff that frequently includes volunteers. Because of these efficiencies, including exemption from income taxes due to their nonprofit status, federally insured credit unions have grown considerably over the past several years. (These institutions also enjoy $100,000 federal deposit (share) insurance.) Problems stemming from inexperienced management and local economic conditions have come with that growth. One risk unique to credit unions is that, when most of its members work for a common employer, or in a single trade, economic difficulties in that one area can quickly turn a large set of loan customers into delinquent nonpayers.

As of January 1, 1990, there were 13,399 federally insured credit unions and approximately 3,000 more that carried no deposit insurance or which had so-called "state" share insurance coverage. In 1980, there were 17,350 federally insured credit unions. While not all of the "charter cancellations" have been failures, enough credit unions have required federal intervention to indicate that this part of the thrift industry could also become part of the overall banking crisis.

Banking in the 1990s: How Present Trends Will Affect Us Through the Decade

While detailed predictions of the future are difficult to make, the implications of current trends can be surmised. For example, consider the following facts. Currently, there is widespread slack demand for real estate across the nation. An estimated average of one property in fourteen is subject to economic distress, thereby motivating the owner to sell. Real estate investment now receives more disfavored tax treatment than previously. The government S&L bailout agency (The Resolution Trust Corporation or RTC) is readying billions of dollars more in real estate for sale, in addition to the $16 billion it already has on the market. In the face of these negative factors, most parts of the country should expect little price appreciation by property anytime soon, unless an exceedingly strong economic boom or severe inflation develops. Since neither of these appears on the horizon, many analysts expect the real estate doldrums to be lengthy, leaving plenty of time for bargain hunters to find choice properties.

Other banking trends could develop as follows:

Bank and S&L Insolvencies

- High failure rates are likely to persist into the early 1990s.
- A recession (if it occurs) will seriously increase and extend banking problems.

- Popular understanding of the limited protection offered by deposit insurance will increase.
- Regulators will continue to tighten their treatment of deposit insurance claims.
- Discussion and debate about leaks in the federal deposit insurance umbrella will become more intense.
- Rude surprises, such as those encountered by twenty-three thousand small account holders who lost all of their money when Lincoln Savings of California was seized by regulators in April 1989, will become more commonplace.

Size and Diversification of the U.S. Banking Industry

- Tendency to shrink modestly will continue.
- U.S. industry will not evolve, like Canadian industry, toward a few dozen megabanks.
- Over twenty thousand institutions (banks, remnant S&Ls and credit unions) should remain intact by the year 2000.

Home Financing

- Fewer S&Ls will mean less competition for the mortgage dollar.
- Higher fees, tougher qualification requirements, more severe appraisals will be the trend.
- Financing costs will become a more important element than they are now in many real estate deals.

Costs of Doing Business with Banks

- Significant new demands by regulators and other government agencies are pushing up bank operating costs dramatically.

- Changing work force composition is driving up labor costs (and diminishing service quality).
- Results will include ballooning fees, reductions in convenience and more difficulty in resolving snafus.

The Challenge

Over the next several years the financial world will see marked increases in customer frustration and resentment. The financially strong banks that can develop policies to simplify customer transactions will be the banks of preference over the next decade. As the issue of safety continues to move toward center stage, forward-looking institutions will seek to reassure and educate their clientele to minimize the risks described in the remaining chapters of this book. Their slower-reacting competitors will lose out as customers take their business elsewhere.

DEPOSIT INSURANCE

Basic Concepts

Any person with deposit accounts in a federally insured financial institution has amounts up to $100,000 "covered" by a U. S. government agency. For banks, the deposit insurance is through the Bank Insurance Fund (BIF) of the Federal Deposit Insurance Corporation (FDIC). For S&Ls, the FDIC-administered Savings Association Insurance Fund (SAIF) provides the coverage. The funds for the insurance coverage come from annual premiums paid by each institution. The premiums run in the vicinity of fifteen to twenty cents per hundred dollars of deposits. Credit union insurance, extended by the National Credit Union Share Insurance Fund (NCUSIF), is paid by special assessment on each institution. However, in recent years, the premiums have been waived because NCUSIF has been deemed by the National Credit Union Administration to possess sufficient funds.

Government officials, including presidents, congressional leaders and banking regulators, have frequently assured the public that the full faith and credit of the U.S. government back these insurance funds. Most experts interpret these assurances to mean that, regardless of the solvency of the insurance funds, somehow, some way, the government will do whatever is necessary to return depositors' money to them.

However, there are situations in which the government's ability to repay depositors could clearly be limited. Some of these situations are discussed later in this chapter.

Additional Coverage

The deposit insurance coverage is $100,000 *per person, per bank*. Certain exceptions, such as use of a joint account plus individual accounts, can extend the coverage to $300,000 per couple. By use of trusts and other special devices, coverage can be extended further to $500,000, but the "fine print" provisions of the deposit insurance policy are especially tricky for these higher coverages.

One example of such tricky fine print is a rule that the FDIC uses to assess whether joint accounts are really joint. In the course of a bank liquidation, when the FDIC prepares to pay off insured depositors, its examination of account paperwork may determine that there is a "dominant" owner of each joint account. If there appears to be an uneven split in ownership, the account will be apportioned between the primary and secondary owner in accordance with the degree of control suggested by the bank's records. The $100,000 limit is then applied. In one case, because a wife had overlooked signing a joint account's signature card, the FDIC imputed ownership of the entire account to her husband. The rationale was that the wife possessed no withdrawal privileges.

In summary, the simplest way to remember the main features of federal deposit insurance is the "rule of ones"—one bank, one person, one hundred thousand dollars.

Common Misconceptions

As stated above, federal deposit insurance is per account owner, not per account. Ordinarily, spreading one's money over several accounts at the same bank provides no additional protection, despite what has been printed in several major news magazines and at least one national daily newspaper. Deposits placed in different branches of the same bank are also combined when the regulators make insurance payout determinations. Use of a different name or a middle initial, or even a separate social security number, does not help either. If the bank fails and is liquidated by the regulators, the deposit insurance payout is decided on the simple basis of "who actually owns the money." All of the accounts owned by one person are added up and paid. If that amount exceeds $100,000, only $100,000 is paid.

Another common misconception is that any financial instrument received in return for money brought into a bank is protected. Only deposits are protected. While most banks do not offer uninsured accounts, enough cases have occurred to warrant caution. Examples are provided in Chapter 4. If you are unsure as to whether or not your account is protected, follow up with your state banking agency or consumer protection office. Be wary if words such as "deposit-like," "as good as deposits," "investment in the bank" or "backed fully by the bank" are used.

In many instances, creditors and other people who are owed money by a failed bank are not protected. In the bankruptcy proceedings that follow many closures, the federal regulators' claims for reimbursement for deposit insurance payouts are given preference over the claims of other, unsecured creditors. Thus, there is usually no chance for any recovery by the other creditors.

Some people have the idea that if they owe a bank money, and the bank fails, the amounts they have on deposit will be used to offset the loan. This is true only if the deposits and loans are with the same corporate entity. When regulators tally deposits and offsetting loans for insurance payout considerations, no consideration is given to a depositor's loan position at separately incorporated subsidiaries or affiliated institutions. For example, if you owe $60,000 to a bank's mortgage corporation or its leasing subsidiary, and have $140,000 on deposit at the bank itself, $40,000 of the deposit total is exposed. If the FDIC liquidates a bank and its subsidiaries, the regulators either sell the loans to another institution or pursue collection directly. In either case, if payments are withheld, repossession or prosecution for nonpayment follows.

Insurance Coverage vs. Kind of Bank

Many people become confused when trying to match a kind of bank with the federal agency, if any, that provides deposit insurance. Frequently, one hears questions like, "My bank is a state bank, does that mean it is not federally insured?" (In fact, it probably is insured by the FDIC.) The source of the confusion is the bank's name. The name usually reflects the nature of the bank's charter. (The charter is the legal document that permits the bank to conduct certain types of business operations, depending upon what kind of bank it is.) The name usually sheds little or no light on the identity of the deposit insurer.

Confusion can also arise because the principal government agency that regulates a financial institution may be different from the agency that is responsible for its deposit insurance. For example, all "national" banks are regulated by the Office of the Comptroller of the Currency, but are insured by the FDIC. Some credit unions are both state regulated and state chartered but are insured by the National Credit Union Administration, a federal agency. The list below identifies the three federal deposit insurance plans and the types of institutions that are insured by each.

Federal Agency Responsible for Deposit Insurance	*Types of Institutions Which May Be Insured By Each Agency*
FDIC Bank Insurance Fund (BIF)	National banks, state banks, banks which are Federal Reserve board members, some savings banks, some cooperative banks, some thrift and loan associations
FDIC Savings Association Insurance Fund (SAIF)	Savings and loan associations, building and loan associations, federal savings banks, some savings banks, some cooperative banks, some thrift and loan associations
National Credit Union Administration Share Insurance Fund (NCUSIF)	Federal credit unions, state credit unions

When a Bank Fails

The mechanics of bank closures are usually set in motion several weeks before the event actually occurs. The regulatory agency responsible assembles a special team, sets a date (often on a Thursday) and begins preparations, all with the highest level of secrecy. Early in the bank's last week, the closing team travels to the city where the bank is located, often spreading out to many motels to avoid detection. On the evening before, selected news media, known for their ability to be discrete, are contacted and advised of the time and place of the closing.

On the final day, usually at the end of normal business hours, the liquidation team assembles, with U.S. marshals, local police and news media, then quickly enters the bank. The lead liquidator announces that the bank is being closed and that all personnel, from that moment on, are employees of the U.S. government. The announcement often generates shock and disbelief among the bank's employees, who often have little idea that the bank is in trouble, let alone a candidate for closure. (For example, just a few weeks before one of the most well-known closings of the 1980s, an officer of Penn Square Bank—taken over by the regulators on July 1, 1982—invested over one million dollars in the bank's stock.) An emotional scene typically follows, in which stunned and crying people are briefed on their responsibilities as public servants and how they are to help the regulators close the bank. Management officials are usually escorted out of the bank immediately. Automatic teller machines are also quickly deactivated.

Recovery of Insured Deposits

Over the weekend that follows, regulators make arrangements for depositors to receive access to their money, usually by transferring the accounts to another bank or, in some cases, preparing to disburse the accounts directly. Out of state account holders are notified by first class mail. To claim their money when a failed institution is liquidated, depositors must fill out an insurance claim form, have it notarized and submit it to the liquidating regulator. If done by mail, normal recovery of deposit account money most often takes several weeks. When the claim is contested by the regulatory authorities, payment can be considerably delayed, if made at all.

In a case involving the failure, in 1985, of the Golden Pacific Bank, located in New York City's Chinatown, a set of disputed "yellow certificates of deposit" were not repaid to customers until 1989. The repayment followed a lengthy court fight between the FDIC and the account holders. The name "yellow CDs" came from the color of the paper the depositors' receipts were printed on. The FDIC could not find records in the bank for the certificates and, on that basis, refused to honor them.

How Longer Recovery Times Can Occur

Although seldom used, banks, and regulators who take over banks, can invoke their right to require a "minimum notice of withdrawal." This means that thirty days notice of the depositor's intention to take out money has to be given. Under some circumstances, including times of "national emergency," state and federal officials can ration the amounts allowed to be withdrawn. They can also postpone withdrawals. Both of these devices have seldom been used since the Great Depression. One instance of a deposit payout deferral that lasted for almost one week occurred when the Sparta-Sanders State Bank in Sparta, Kentucky, was closed on April 18, 1983. The bank's former management obtained a court injunction to keep the FDIC from liquidating the accounts.

Rationing of withdrawal amounts was imposed for a short time during the 1962 closure of a West Virginia bank. Recent, more widespread cases of rationing applied to curb withdrawal activity when federal deposit insurance was not involved are discussed later in this chapter.

Actions by the Regulators
to Limit Deposit Insurance Coverage

Due to the heavy drain on federal deposit insurance funds in recent years, banking regulators have begun to take a stance on payouts that is more usually associated with private insurers. They examine all claims and disqualify those that do not meet every aspect of the deposit insurance policy requirements. Sometimes they can be very exacting: for example, when checks in transit at the time a bank is closed have been dishonored and used to bring a customer's total account balance above $100,000. In fairness, it must be added that, so far, payment of deposit insurance claims has usually been very prompt in comparison with delays by private sector insurance companies.

A recent legislative measure reduces deposit insurance coverage for special cases that qualify for more than the $100,000 limit. One of the provisions of the 1989 S&L bailout bill calls for "unifying" the deposit insurance policies of the different federal banking regulatory agencies. These provisions have resulted in a tightening of the rules to the strictest possible version. Their impact affects certain combinations of joint, fiduciary, custodial, testimentory, IRA, Keogh and other specialty accounts. A full description was printed in the Federal Register on December 21, 1989. Copies of the eighteen-page document may also be available from the FDIC's legal division. It is designated as FIL-25, dated 12/28/89.

Another recent policy change put forth by the FDIC is curtailment of pension plan deposit insurance coverage. Although political reaction may force the agency to back down, as of this writing, the FDIC has announced its intention to apply the $100,000 limit to certain pension plans (called "457" plans) as if the plan were for a single person. These plans typically provide for employees of state and local governments and nonprofit agencies. Previously the policy had been to cover all pension plans in the amount of $100,000 for each of the plan participants. With many pension plan members locked into their employer's plan or otherwise caught by provisions that preclude a fast exit, the prospect looms that some may have their pensions wiped out by bank failures.

Situations in Which the Government's Deposit Insurance May Not Be Able to Repay Depositors

Currently, the FDIC's Bank Insurance Fund has gross assets near $14 billion. Because a portion of this money is tied up in failed banks, the amount available for payouts is somewhat less. Since insured deposits at all banks total $2.1 trillion, the Bank Insurance Fund possesses considerably less than one cent per dollar of insured deposits. Viewed another way, failures of moderately large banks, such as Continental Illinois Bank in 1984, or First Republic Bank of Texas in 1988, typically cost the FDIC $4 billion to $6 billion. Thus, the Bank Insurance Fund could be strained by several such failures in a short period. If such strains should occur, the Federal Reserve will most likely make money available in an attempt to control the crisis—a crisis that would surely be set off by such a string of large bank failures. (This is not just a theoretical possibility. During the past several years, the Federal Reserve has quickly provided money to a number of banks and S&Ls to halt runs before they could get out of hand.)

The 1985 Ohio and Maryland crises, with so-called state insured S&Ls, illustrated how widespread runs on federally insured institutions might be controlled. In those states, the private deposit insurance did not have sufficient funds to pay off depositors at failed institutions. When it became known that there was no state backing for the insolvent deposit insurance fund, runs began at other S&Ls. State officials quickly declared a "bank holiday" and closed all of the then-uninsured S&Ls in the state. Within a few weeks the still-solvent S&Ls were reopened but withdrawal limitations of $500 to $700 per month were imposed. Although most of the depositors eventually got their money (years later), many suffered hardship, especially those who had committed downpayments to transactions involving a penalty for not following through in a timely fashion. Home purchases are examples of such transactions.

How the Government Could Change Present Deposit Insurance Payout Policies

As stated earlier, if necessary, the government can avoid making good on deposit insurance claims simply by delaying them. Bank holidays have long been recognized as a means to put a hold on widespread panic. Since an open-ended deferral on the availability of people's money could cause political (as well as civil) tumult, and since the rationing approach in two states quickly led to relative calm, this alternative appears to be a likely future tool. Another attractive feature of rationing withdrawals is its face-saving political stance. Few, if any, of the government's assurances to insured account holders have ever included commitments to speedy refunds.

Other, more sinister responses to a deposit insurance crisis that could be adopted by cynical lawmakers include

- Forcing depositors to accept long-term, low-interest-rate U.S. government bonds or notes

- Adjusting the tax code to treat deposit account closings as casualty losses in the year the bank is closed, and insurance reimbursements as later-year income
- Synchronizing repayment delays to periods of high inflation so that the value of the deposit account refunds, when finally received, is sharply reduced

All of the foregoing maneuvers would still allow the assertion "No one has ever lost a dime of insured deposits" to continue to be made with legalistic correctness.

Relative Strength of the Three Federal Deposit Insurance Funds

As explained above, the strength of federal deposit insurance does not lie in the size of the reserves, but rather in the government's repeated pledges to stand behind each of the funds in case of trouble. Since these pledges have yet to be seriously tested, the question is often asked, "How do the reserves in the deposit insurance funds compare with the amounts they could possibly be called upon to pay?" The amounts are broken down below.

Federal Deposit Insurance	Estimated Balance of Fund as of 12/31/89	Estimated Insured Deposits (or Shares) as of 12/31/89	Insurance Fund Reserves per Dollar of Insured Deposits
FDIC Bank Insurance Fund (BIF)	$13.7 billion	$2.2 trillion	0.6 cents
FDIC Savings Association Insurance Fund (SAIF)	None	$975 billion	0.0 cents

Federal Deposit Insurance	Estimated Balance of Fund as of 12/31/89	Estimated Insured Deposits (or Shares) as of 12/31/89	Insurance Fund Reserves per Dollar of Insured Deposits
National Credit Union Share Insurance Fund (NCUSIF)	$2.0 billion	$165 billion	1.3 cents

It should be kept in mind that the insurance reserves given above are "gross" values. That is, they count money that may be tied up and not available to pay depositors, should a quick need arise. The federal deposit insurance agencies are usually tight-lipped about the actual amounts in the funds that are "liquid," or ready to be drawn upon immediately. However, private estimates are that between $4 billion and $8 billion of the Bank Insurance Fund is tied up in the ownership of, or loans to, reconstituted banks.

The Savings Association Insurance Fund (SAIF), which just received its start in late 1989 following the widely headlined insolvency of its forerunner, the Federal Savings and Loan Insurance Corporation, is not slated to receive any money until 1992. Instead, the premiums paid by the S&Ls are being used to fund the ongoing thrift bailout. In this environment, savings and loan association depositors must look to government promises and guarantees rather than the current, nonexistent reserves of SAIF.

The National Credit Union Share Insurance Fund, recapitalized in 1984 after having problems keeping up with failures in that industry, also is not as liquid as the total in the table would indicate. For example, among the fund's assets is a $2 million mortgage on the building used by the National Credit Union Administration.

"State" Deposit Insurance Funds

Over the past two hundred years, there have been numerous deposit insurance plans set up by trade groups of financial institutions or state banking authorities. The reason for these plans, like the federal deposit insurance, has been to eliminate or sharply reduce the tendency for bank runs to develop. These deposit insurance attempts have been beset by two problems. One has been a lack of sufficient funds held in reserve to cover more than the failure of a few small banks. The other has been the unwillingness of the state or federal government to stand behind a plan once it gets into trouble. The 1985 Maryland and Ohio debacles typify the situation with nonfederal plans. Despite impressive names like Maryland Savings Share Insurance Corporation (MSSIC) and Ohio Guaranty Fund, there was no state support for thousands of depositors in insolvent thrifts in those states. (Later, in 1989, Maryland recognized its obligation and paid depositors there.) Less widely reported, but equally traumatic to the families that lost their savings, was the collapse, in 1983, of the Nebraska Depository Institution Guarantee Corporation.

In addition to the widespread coverage by the FDIC's Bank Insurance Fund (BIF) and Savings Association Insurance Fund (SAIF), some institutions have "excess FDIC coverage" under the auspices of plans provided by various banking associations. For example, the Massachusetts Central Fund provides deposit insurance "without any limit" to account holders in that state's savings banks. The fund, like other private deposit insurance, could cover only a few moderate-sized failures. Furthermore, state officials emphatically decline to pledge "full faith and credit" of the state as backing to the fund. Similar situa-

29

tions prevail in Pennsylvania, North Carolina and several other states.

Currently, most serious depositors ignore the additional coverage that the so-called state insurance funds provide. Instead, they direct their strategies to maximizing their coverage under the federal plans.

Uninsured Institutions

Although most banking institutions in the U.S. have either the BIF, SAIF or NCUSIF insurance, there are a number of banks, "near-banks" and "non-banks" that do not. Categories of non–federally insured financial institutions are listed below.

- Ordinary state-chartered (old) banks that did not have to join the FDIC because they qualified for certain "grandfathering" provisions when the FDIC was formed in 1934; less than a few dozen of these remain.
- Commercial credit companies that allow "deposit participation" in their activities; hundreds, perhaps thousands, of these finance companies exist nationwide. They are usually small, family-owned operations that specialize in personal lending.
- Privately insured or non-insured credit unions; there are approximately three thousand of these institutions.
- "Private" banks, somewhat rare institutions that specialize in providing very personalized financial services to upscale clients; many are federally insured, a few are not.
- Limited service or "non-bank" banks, a development of the last five years, formed to pursue activities relating to the securities industry; there

are several dozen of these institutions, some of which take in ''deposits'' and offer services similar to checking accounts.

Precautions You Can Take

Federal deposit insurance, despite its risks and limitations, is the last line of defense most of us have against bank failure. Although it may be obvious, many people and businesses have lost money by not observing the following two rules.

1. Be sure your institution is BIF, SAIF or NCUSIF insured. If you do not see one of these three symbols displayed prominently, ask why. If you ask and are made to feel uncomfortable for asking, the institution probably is not federally insured. Bank failures have become so prominent in the modern financial landscape that now all bankers in the country understand (or should understand) the reasonable worries that their depositors have.

2. Be sure that *your account is also federally insured*. If you are in doubt, try to get your bank representative to put it in writing. (This may be difficult, especially for small amounts, simply because busy customer representatives may not want to bother, or may be reluctant to make assurances that they do not completely understand.) Your state or local consumer protection agency may be able to help.

Accounts Over $100,000

One strategy is obvious—spread your money over many banks, never putting more than $100,000 in each. If you must invest $100,000 (for example, to take advantage of an attractive jumbo CD rate), have the interest sent to you or deposited into your account at a different bank, at the most frequent intervals possible. That way, the least possible amount of interest is at risk.

Joint accounts provide an easy way to extend coverage to $300,000. But the subtleties of current deposit insurance claim-settlement procedures should be understood before committing funds beyond $100,000. Also, all depositors with more than $100,000 in an institution need to be continually alert to rules changes that could place them at a disadvantage. In comparison to most government deposit insurance officials, anyone with over $100,000 of banked assets is quite well off. Large account holders should expect little sympathy from federal banking liquidators or deposit insurance adjusters. These officials usually possess personal accounts totaling well under the $100,000 limit. Indeed, one can expect to encounter the attitude "We have to insure you, but it is your responsibility to follow all of the rules for the insurance to work."

Trust accounts, IRAs, Keogh Plans and other combinations of account types can extend coverage to as much as $500,000 for a couple. Needless to say, considerable caution is indicated in the structuring of such arrangements, the considerations for which extend well beyond the scope of this book.

Additional Lines of Defense

One lesson from the Ohio and Maryland crises is that different kinds of banking institutions may be affected in different ways should federal deposit insurance get into trouble, or if the government should declare "bank holidays." Large depositors and small account holders alike should spread their funds over various types of institutions, rather than simply choosing different institutions of the same kind. For example, diversification among banks, S&Ls and credit unions, as well as some non-bank investments, can be a prudent course. Many careful people also keep a cash contingency fund on hand, sufficient to cover a month of living expenses. Some people also maintain an additional three months of "liquidity" distributed over

- A charge card or two at a bank other than their regular bank
- A checking account at a bank other than the one at which they keep their savings
- A credit union share account
- A money market fund (not a bank; not federally insured) with check writing privileges

Watching for Trouble

Increasingly, many account holders, and others who could be hurt by their banks' failure, are not relying solely on the backstop of federal deposit insurance. It is becoming more commonplace for private citizens and businesses alike to watch for indications that their financial institutions could be in trouble. They want to be able to take appropriate action before matters get to the deposit insurance claim stage.

Newspaper stories are often a tip-off that all is not well at a bank or S&L, particularly if the institution is prominent. However, by the time a bank's troubles have reached the press, it is often too late to do much more than watch the final drama unfold. There are other ways you can learn, early on, about your bank's condition. The next chapter explains how to identify and evaluate this information.

3

FINANCIAL INSTITUTIONS IN TROUBLE: WARNING SIGNALS

The Art of Doublespeak

Suppose, tomorrow, you receive the following letter from your S&L or bank.

Dear Mr. or Ms._____:

As you know, Federal First Savings and Loan has grown with this community since 1934. Recently, as part of our ongoing effort to provide our customers with the best service possible, Federal First has joined the Resolution Trust Corporation's conservatorship program. We are excited about this new step, which adds one more aspect to the safety of your funds here. More information about our participation in this important federal program will follow soon. Meanwhile, we urge you to check into our special high yield money market account. . . .

While the letter is fictitious, the concept behind it is not. Would you instantly recognize this as a message that your institution had been taken over by the federal agency whose sole purpose is the liquidation of failed or failing thrifts? Would the soothing phrases and slick style cause your eyes to glaze over as you quickly sent the letter to the trash can—without understanding its concealed message? The message, of course, is that now, or soon, you may be required to "apply" to have your money returned.

Public relations experts know that one of the most effective ways to keep an uproar from developing over an organization's controversial policies and actions is to fully disclose what is occurring, but in such uninteresting terms that the message is ignored. Examples of such creative disclosure abound. Your school's announcement that your child will be participating in their college-track level program sounds great—until months or years later, when you learn that they really meant your youngster had been excluded from the top-ranking "honors" program. An illustrative case from the U.S. Defense Department was a statement about "delivery of a physics package." In that instance, the "package" was an intercontinental missile flight carrying a live nuclear warhead. Perhaps the Central Intelligence Agency is the best master at using understatement to avoid attention. Unless told otherwise, an outsider who does not read spy novels would never know that "to end an operation with prejudice" means killing the participants.

What Do Your Bank's Announcements Really Mean?

Banking institutions and their government regulators are also well versed in breaking bad news gently. Their motivation is simple. They do not want investors to unload their stock holdings, suppliers to tighten up credit, customers to flee or runs to start. Fortunately, it is possible to read between the lines of news articles and direct mail messages. Ask the following questions:

1. What is the single most important piece of information that the announcement or news story conveys?

2. If the story was disclosed by the institution's management, why?

3. Is the heart of the message good news or bad news? Note that news is never neutral.

4. If the message has not been made easy for you to understand, why not?

5. Does the message seem unusually boring, considering the degree of trouble the source has taken to put it in front of you?

6. What action does the source want you to take or avoid?

How Some Common Words and Phrases Should Be Interpreted

Perhaps the best example of understatement used in the financial world today is the word "troubled." In most cases, by the time that word finds its way into use by responsible media, the institution it describes is either close to failing or, at the least, severely threatened. "Restructuring" is another key word that should raise a flag. If an institution is restructuring its assets, that often means it is scrambling to sell whatever it can to raise money as quickly as it can. Similarly, news of management restructuring or realignment often indicates demotions and firings resulting from performance disasters. An "earnings downturn" can mean anything from lower profits than in the previous reporting period, to solvency-threatening losses. A few other terms that often indicate problems include:

Flat earnings—Often indicates no profit at all. (A one percent return on assets is considered nominal in banking.)

One-time losses—May recur if the source of the losses is bad loans. (The key question is what happens in quarters following "one-time" losses.)

Loan loss provision—Acknowledgment by bank management that more loans are going sour. (It is a good bet that future write-offs will be at least as bad as current provisions.)

International operations—Foreign loans or sources of deposits. (How much of their money comes from foreign deposits and goes to foreign loans?)

Nonperforming assets—Bad loans and foreclosed real estate. (How do these amounts compare with equity and loan loss reserves?)

Conservatorship—Takeover by federal regulators preparatory to liquidation or a government-financed merger with a healthy institution. (This is not a beneficial development!)

Assistance transaction—Money from federal regulators to keep a failing institution afloat. (This situation was previously called a failure.)

Forebearance—Permission by regulators for an institution to remain open despite its failure to meet minimum financial safety requirements, usually related to how closely it is allowed to approach the edge of insolvency. (An institution that has been granted regulatory forebearance is shaky indeed.)

Consent agreement—A formal document in which bank management promises to accomplish some specific degree of improvement by a particular date. (Failure to meet the goal often means the end of the bank.)

How to Get More Information

If you receive indications that your bank or S&L may not be in the best of health, or if you simply want to investigate its status, several sources are available.

Banks and S&Ls are required to publish periodically (usually once each year) a "statement of condition." These typically appear in a local newspaper. Also, commercial banks and S&Ls must make an "annual disclosure statement" available on request. The information is also often printed in small brochures and distributed in banks' and S&Ls' lobbies for customers to pick up. While these statements can be difficult to understand, and often omit important income and problem loan information, they can provide useful indications of a bank's condition.

In addition, every federally insured financial institution must provide detailed, in-depth financial reports to its regulators every three months (six months for credit unions). These reports, known as "call reports," can be obtained from the appropriate regulatory agencies through the National Technical Information Service, 5285 Port Royal Road, Springfield, VA 22161, (703) 487–4650. The cost is about $25 per report, and some expertise is required to understand the information.

The Federal Financial Institutions Examination Council, or FFIEC, provides reports on individual banks and contrasts them with similar-sized "peer group" banks. The "uniform bank performance reports" cost $30 per bank and may be ordered from UBPR, Dept. 4320, Chicago, IL 60673, (800) 843–1669. Checks should be made payable to the FFIEC.

Several private sector firms also provide data and analysis. Sheshunoff and Company, One Texas Center, 505 Barton Spring Road, Austin, TX 78704, (512) 472–2244, offers call report data and analysis information in a variety of forms, including a CD ROM which contains all of the banks in the country with information reaching back for five years. The annual cost is $10,000 and includes quarterly updates. Discounts apply to orders involving multiple products.

Keefe, Bruyette and Woods, Inc., specialists in Bank Securities, offer a wide range of information. They are located at Two World Trade Center, New York, NY 10048, (212) 323–8383. Among their products is the Keefe Bankbook, which, for $500, provides comparative performance analysis of the 297 largest public holding companies and their securities.

Another private sector provider of information about banks is the credit rating agency Dun and Bradstreet (D&B), One Imperial Way, Allentown, PA 18195, (800) 879–1362. Their Dun's Express Report (payable by credit card) is $60.

Our firm, VERIBANC, Inc., specializes in furnishing easy-to-understand ratings on each of the country's thirty thousand banks, S&Ls and credit unions. Reports range from instant telephone safety ratings (paid for by credit card), at $10 for the first institution and $3 for each additional institution rated at the same time, to in-depth research reports ($45). More information about VERIBANC, (800) 442–2657, is provided on the last page.

A different type of data, the highest interest rates paid to depositors, is offered by the publication 100 Highest Yields, P.O. Box 088888, North Palm Beach, FL, 33408, (800) 327–7717. The cost of the weekly publication is $98 per year.

Talk to Your Banker

One of the best potential sources of information is the management of your bank. A frank discussion, particularly if you are forearmed with facts that you have derived from the sources listed above, can be illuminating. Frequently, just the reaction of bank personnel to your concern conveys a message. You will know that your bank has nothing to hide if the bank official responds to your query with "Yes, we had a small loss last quarter because we had to charge off some real estate loans. However, if you have the time to look with me at our latest quarter's call report, which we just sent in, you can see that the bank has returned to profitability. Our capital is well above regulatory minimums and industry norms, and our few remaining problem loans are well covered by current reserves."

On the other hand, some responses can confirm your fears. Examples include "We do not discuss the bank's private financial matters" or "Sure, we are insolvent, but so are hundreds of other institutions. Since the government will be taking care of the problem anyway, you need not worry." The latter quote was actually spoken by one S&L representative. Needless to say, worry is particularly appropriate in such a case. A candid admission of insolvency by a banker is probably the most telling information you can obtain about a financial institution.

Three Specific Tests

While you can order reports that show the results of safety tests on an institution's financial condition, you can also perform a checkup on any bank by yourself. Each of the three tests described in the following paragraphs examines a critical part of an institution's operations. Over the last several years, virtually no institution that has been closed by regulators has "passed" all three tests. (The few failures that did leak through the tests with good scores gave fraudulent or falsified data on their reports, or were subject to exceedingly unusual circumstances.) For example, in 1989, of the 207 banks that failed, 204 of them missed at least one of the requirements outlined below. Taken together, the three tests are a good way to predict an institution's future financial health.

Test One: Does Your Institution Have Adequate Capital?

A financial institution such as a bank, S&L or credit union does business by lending out money that it has borrowed from its depositors. Thus, its business is controlling investments of other people's funds. In addition, it uses (and, of course, controls) money and other items of value that belong to the institution's owners. This portion is called equity, also often referred to as capital. The total of the institution's equity plus the investments that really belong to others is called assets.

It is both good business practice and a federal requirement for financial institutions to have a stake in the monies they control; in other words, a certain percentage of their assets must consist of equity. In fact, if the equity of an institution drops to zero or less, the institution is "insolvent." For this reason, equity is often referred to as a financial cushion. It allows an institution to withstand temporary periods of unprofitability without having to go out of business.

To start our first test, obtain from your bank, savings and loan association or credit union a copy of its latest "statement of condition." This may also be called a counter statement, a balance sheet or a financial summary. Sometimes larger banks simply distribute copies of their annual report. If you are using the latter, find the page that is called "consolidated balance sheet" or a similar name. You can also use an institution's quarterly "call report."

The key word to look for is "assets." Under this heading, you will find a list of the bank's different assets and amounts in each assets category. The information you need is often at the bottom, next to the heading "Total Assets." This is usually the largest amount of money given on the page.

Now, if your institution is an ordinary bank, you will need to find an item called "equity," "shareholders' equity" or "total equity." If you are examining a savings and loan association, this item is called "net worth." If your bank has the word "Mutual" in its name, there will not be an entry on the balance sheet for equity or net worth. In that case, find, near the bottom of the page, the amount given for "surplus." Whatever this item is called— equity, net worth or surplus—divide it by the "total assets" and express the result as a percentage.

If the result exceeds 5 percent, the institution's equity is above usual norms for financial institutions and, unless it has severe difficulties with problem loans (see test three, which follows), is not likely to be receiving strong regulatory scrutiny. A ratio between 6 percent and 7.5 percent is considered quite good. Above 7.5 percent is superb.

If equity is between 3 and 5 percent of assets, the institution may be considered weak. However, some regulatory authorities allow the institutions under their jurisdiction to operate with equity as low as 3 percent of assets (S&Ls, for example). If the equity-to-assets ratio is below 3 percent, the institution is almost surely receiving considerable attention from its regulatory authorities. The reason why its equity is so low certainly deserves your close attention too.

Needless to say, if the institution's equity is negative (often indicated by a number printed within parentheses), you know immediately that it is insolvent. Only recently, with the federal banking regulatory system overloaded by the crisis, have insolvent banking institutions continued to operate for very long.

Of course, measures of capital other than equity are used. Among them is tangible net worth, which involves the subtraction of goodwill and other intangible assets from equity before forming the ratio with assets. Currently, S&Ls are required to possess tangible net worth that is at least 1.5 percent of assets (rising to 3 percent of assets by 1994).

Another recently introduced measure is risk-based capital. Risk-based capital requirements account for the varying degrees of safety among different kinds of assets owned by the bank.

Test Two: Is Your Institution Losing Money?

Even though earning money is the purpose of any business, profitability can sometimes be elusive. Banking, like any other endeavor, encounters difficulties that cause institutions to suffer losses. One way of measuring the seriousness of the losses is to pose the question "How long could the present rate of loss continue before the institution's equity would be used up?''

For this test, you will need to look at the ''income'' portion of your financial institution's statement. The income statement is usually presented separately from the balance sheet information used in Test One, above. For many institutions, it is presented on another page. The name for this table of figures is usually ''Statement of Income,'' ''Report of Income,'' ''Income and Expenses,'' ''Statement of Operations'' or some similarly worded item.

First look toward the bottom of the income statement and find the entry for net income. Note whether or not this item is negative or is set within parentheses. (Recall that parentheses designate a loss.) If the institution is profitable, it can be considered to have ''passed'' the income test. Otherwise, copy the amount of net loss the institution suffered.

The other important item you will need from the income statement is the period of time over which the statement applies. This is usually one year, but sometimes the most recent six months or three months of income is presented. Be sure to record the appropriate number of months with the loss figure you copied above.

You will now want to examine how serious the institution's losses are. Divide the net loss figure (you can drop the parentheses or negative sign) by the number of months over which the loss accumulated (the second figure you copied). This will establish the average rate of loss per month over the period.

Now, divide the average rate of loss per month into the same equity amount you used in Test One. The result is the number of months over which the institution can continue to sustain such losses before it runs out of equity. If the institution should continue to lose money at the same rate (it may or may not, of course), it could become insolvent in the number of months you have just calculated.

If the number of months is twelve or less, the losses are clearly quite serious. On the other hand, if the institution could tolerate losses this large for more than a year, the losses are somewhat less threatening.

Test Three: Can Problem Loans Sink Your Institution?

Test One and Two indicate your institution's actual condition as of the date of its financial statement. In addition, the amount of money that an institution has lent, but for which repayment is late or in doubt, needs to be considered. Many institutions keep loan loss reserves to provide a first line of defense against borrowers who default. Thus, the amount of problem loans, in excess of an institution's loan loss reserve, measures the potential degree to which its equity could suffer due to future loan losses. Problem loans can be a better indication of what may lie ahead than actual current amounts of equity and earnings. This test has more of a ''What does the future hold?'' flavor than Tests One and Two.

All of the data needed for this test usually are not available in the small financial statements or newspaper tables that the bank issues. You will need either an annual report, a specially issued ''disclosure report'' or the call report. To begin, you will need to add up the institution's problem loans. These will typically include loans that are seriously past due (usually ninety days or more), loans in nonaccrual condition (unlikely to be repaid) and loans that have been restructured (because of the borrowers' difficulty in repaying). Add these items up to obtain the bank's total problem loans.

Then, find the item called ''loan loss reserves'' or ''balance of reserve for loan losses.'' Compare the loan loss reserve balance with the total problem loans above. If the

46

loan loss reserves exceed the total problem loans, the institution passes this test so easily that no further calculations are needed.

However, if total problem loans exceed loan loss reserves, it is important to know how much the excess is. Subtract the loan loss reserves from the total problem loans to obtain the excess problem loans. Compare excess problem loans to equity (the same amount used in Test One). If excess problem loans exceed equity, the institution could be headed toward insolvency. In other words, if all of the problem loans turn out to be completely worthless, it would take more equity than is available at the bank to make up for the losses involved.

To see how large a bite the problem loans could take out of equity, subtract excess problem loans from equity to obtain discounted equity. Divide discounted equity by total assets and express the result as a percentage. If the result is less than 4 percent, the situation is sufficiently serious that the regulators could be paying close attention to the institution.

Test Summary and a Caution

Three tests for a banking institution's financial health are

1. Is its equity more than 5 percent of assets?
2. Did it have positive net income (i.e., operate profitably) recently?
3. Are its problem loans in excess of its loan loss reserve, and, if so, is this excess serious enough to reduce equity below 4 percent of assets?

If an institution passes all three tests, its odds for continued survival are better than 4,000 to 1. If the tests provide mixed results, i.e., a combination of passes and fails, varying conclusions can be drawn about the institution's safety.

However, in applying the three tests, you should keep two things in mind. One is that conditions may change. Thus, up-to-date financial information is important. The other is that the tests are not infallible. They measure only three (admittedly very important) aspects of a financial institution's operations. Other, normally less important factors can take center stage when circumstances are right. If you observe other signs that an institution is having serious financial problems, do not ignore them just because the numbers from the three tests look good.

Other Signals That Problem Banks Sometimes Display

Detecting financial weakness in a bank, S&L or credit union can be an art as much as a science. In addition to the analytical tools described in the foregoing sections, you can use your intuition when evaluating a bank's safety. For example, the following events should arouse your suspicions:

- Frequent news stories of irregularities, firings, changes of auditors, criticized commercial transactions, etc.
- Ongoing media discussion of the presence of, or repeated visits by, regulatory officials, bank examiners or similar authorities.
- Persistent rumors repeating a theme of financial problems.
- Reorganization of top management, particularly if there have been other reorganizations in the recent past.

- Announcements of new stock offerings, especially if the reasons for the new issue are vague, for example "recapitalization."
- The institution is new. New banks, S&Ls and credit unions have many of the same problems encountered by other kinds of new business. Their greater risk of "not making it" is well known to regulatory authorities, who tend to watch young institutions more closely.

How Often Does a Bank's Health Need to Be Checked?

The simple answer is continuously. Insofar as possible, you should always "have your antenna up" to receive signals about the safety of the institutions with which you bank. These signals can come from friends, newscasts or even from the bank. Relying too heavily on financial data alone could cause you to miss important problem signals. Nonetheless, numbers tell a very strong story even within normal limits on the availability and freshness of financial data. Banks and S&Ls file new financial reports with their regulators every three months. It takes the regulatory authorities another three to four months to release the data to the public. Thus, for example, data from the quarter ending December 31 typically becomes available around April 15.

This delay is not as serious as it might first appear. For example, the three tests discussed earlier in this chapter are based on data that is available to the public before institutions actually fail. Our studies have shown that decline at an institution often occurs slowly enough that there is time to find out and act before the regulators do. If you keep up to date with your bank's financial health on a quarterly basis, you are working with the latest "hard" information available.

The foregoing observations are based upon how long it often takes downturns to set in at healthy banks. When dealing with an institution that you know is already shaky, you need to follow the press and any other information sources continuously. You should review your options and alternatives according to a predefined schedule, at least monthly.

RISKS YOU FACE
IN DEALING WITH BANKS

Customers can suffer serious financial losses when their banks, S&Ls or credit unions run into trouble. Until recently, bank failures were so rare that the cracks in the deposit insurance system simply did not receive widespread attention. For example, in 1982, when the First National Bank of Mount Pleasant, Iowa, failed, and many of the residents of that small town confidently brought their passbooks into the FDIC liquidation receiver, they were shocked and dismayed to find that their accounts were not considered to be ''deposits,'' and therefore were not insured. Later, in 1985, a similar situation occurred in New York City's Chinatown. This episode, described in more detail in Chapter 2, received little attention outside of the New York City area.

In 1989, nearly five hundred federally insured institutions failed. As a result, news coverage of bank failures has increased markedly. For example, the travails of the victims of Charles Keating's Lincoln Savings of Los Angeles's uninsured ''sub debt'' were well reported nationwide. By now, many consumers of banking services are aware that banking can be a risky business. This chapter outlines the wide-ranging set of risks facing anyone involved in a bank failure.

Is Your Bank Really an S&L in Disguise?

As the S&L part of the banking crisis worsened, and the government acknowledged that the S&L deposit insurance had no financial backing, people abandoned that industry in droves. During 1989 alone, deposits totaling over $75 billion were removed from savings and loan associations, in many cases driven away by requirements, imposed by regulators, that S&Ls shrink. Needless to say, S&L bankers tried to stem this tide. Many changed their names so they sounded more banklike. MeraBank, A Federal Savings Bank (formerly First Federal Savings and Loan Association of Arizona), is a typical example. A few even changed their charters so they "really are banks," as one banker put it. However, regardless of what they are called, the key attribute that distinguishes banks from S&Ls is the source of their deposit insurance coverage.

If the FDIC's Bank Insurance Fund (BIF) provides the deposit insurance, the institution is a bank. However, if the insurance is backed by SAIF (a separate, moneyless fund also administered by the FDIC), the firm is an S&L. As this is written, SAIF possesses no reserves. Future premium assessments on S&Ls, which normally would infuse money into the fund, have already been earmarked to pay for part of the bailout of insolvent thrifts. In a word, the only protection for S&L depositors is the government's word.

Risks to Small Depositors

Non-Deposits. Patrons with less than $100,000 in a federally insured institution are insured if their funds with the bank are categorized as "deposits." Examples of items that are *not* deposits include repurchase agreements and subordinated debentures (also known as "sub debt" or "lobby debt"). Some institutions have plans by which customers can purchase U.S. Treasury bills, notes and bonds. Money market mutual funds operated by banks are also uninsured. One example is the Liberty Fund offered by Boston's State Street Bank. It is important to note that if the bank is the registered holder of any of these instruments, its obligation to repay you is *not insured*. If you have Treasury securities, remember that the government's guarantee to redeem them is to the owner designated in government records. If you are that owner, and the bank's role is simply that of a broker or caretaker, you should be able to recover your due. But if, in the eyes of the U.S. Treasury, the bank is the owner of the security, then you could incur a significant loss if the bank failed.

Limited Access to Your Funds. As observed in Chapter 2, banking regulators have several defenses in their arsenals against bank runs. For example, they can close a bank until the crisis settles down. Such "bank holidays" can be brief or lengthy. Regulators can also impose monthly withdrawal limits and extend or postpone deposit insurance settlements.

Lost Interest. Interest and principal are together insured up to $100,000. However, in certain situations, your interest can be treated separately (to your disadvantage). Perhaps you own certificates of deposit or similar accounts in which you have agreed to keep a certain amount of money at the bank for a certain length of time (usually from one to five years). In return, the bank has agreed to pay you a specified rate of interest on the deposit, usually somewhat higher than is being paid for accounts that allow the customer to make withdrawals anytime. If you want to retrieve the money before the end of the agreed upon period, the bank may refuse. More likely, however, they will accommodate you but will levy a penalty. Typical penalties are the forfeiture of from three months to one year of interest or, if the account has just been opened, up to 10 percent of the amount deposited.

Problems also arise when institutions fail and the regulators transfer these "time deposit" accounts to healthier banks. To encourage healthy institutions to help pick up the pieces from the failures, regulators allow acquiring institutions to lower the interest rates on the accounts that they take in this manner. When rates are lowered, you, the depositor, are supposed to be given the option of removing your money. Typically the new institution will advise you by first-class mail that your account now resides at a different bank and give you two weeks to notify them that you want to remove your funds. If they do not hear from you, they assume that you accept the new interest rate.

Difficulties can occur if the letter is delayed in the mail or if the account holder is traveling and does not receive the letter before the end of the two week time period. This procedure can also be troublesome if the depositor lives in another state and disagrees with the new bank about the timeliness of the notification. (Depositors at remote locations may not even see news coverage of the failure of a faraway institution.)

In a few cases, bank representatives have told depositors that they simply were not allowed to remove their funds before the maturity date of their original deposit agreement. While such a statement probably would not stand if challenged, resolving such a problem can be difficult and expensive. Imagine if you had a time deposit that had several years yet to run, and the interest rate was suddenly cut by one-third. Then, suppose your banker, in effect, said to you, "You cannot have your money, or you must pay a whopping penalty; if you do not like it, then sue me." Consider, too, how much worse it would be if your bank were several hundreds or thousands of miles away.

CDs Purchased on the Secondary Market. A subtle risk faces investors who purchase their certificates of deposit (CDs) on the secondary market (i.e., from a brokerage firm or other third party). In one case, a dentist paid a purchase premium for a five-year, 13.4 percent–yield CD that had been issued two years earlier. At the time he bought the CD, rates were near 7.5 percent. With his purchase premium, the effective yield at maturity would have been near 9 percent. Unfortunately, when the issuing institution failed, and the deposit insurance paid principal and accrued interest, the purchase premium was not covered. In this case, the unsuspecting dentist lost $9,000 on a CD that in the month prior to the institution's failure had been worth $52,000.

Two rules to be followed when purchasing CDs that have already been issued to someone else are

1. Be sure that the institution responsible for the underlying value of a CD security is healthy.
2. Take special care if the price of a deposit-insured security includes a purchase premium. Be aware that the premium portion is not insured.

Lost Checks. A different kind of risk has emerged as many banks have begun microfilming or digitizing their customers' canceled checks. The checks are discarded, and in principle, the account holder can obtain a copy of the check upon special order to the bank. Of course, there is a fee for this service.

Problems crop up when a bank fails or is sold and the backup check records are lost or thrown away. (Even

55

healthy banks have been known to destroy check records after as little as one year.) What if you need your canceled check to prove you paid an important bill? The Internal Revenue Service could audit you and require you to prove past expenditures. If your bank is gone, and you do not have canceled checks, you may well be out of luck. (Depending upon circumstances, you may be able to access records of your check through the Federal Reserve's clearing system. To follow up, inquire at your nearest Federal Reserve bank.)

The entire risk of lost checks can be avoided by using bank wire to provide the ultimate in security and documented proof of payment. For a fee that runs near $15, you get nearly instantaneous transmission and a receipt showing "finality" of your payment.

Little-Known Risks to Large Depositors

The holder of an account totaling more than $100,000 is typically more skilled in avoiding weak institutions than is the small depositor. However, the following areas can be overlooked by people managing large amounts of money, when they assess their deposit risk exposure.

Escrow Accounts. In liquidations, the FDIC counts moneys standing in escrow accounts toward the $100,000 insurance limit. If you have moderate real estate holdings, your pool of tax and insurance escrow payments could be significant.

Checks in Transit. After closing a bank, the FDIC will refuse to honor checks that have not been cashed prior to the bank's failure. If payees are slow to cash checks or if intermediate routing banks are slow in presenting checks for payment, your account's combination of checks outstanding and funds on deposit could reach unexpectedly high levels. (This situation cannot occur when payments are made by bank wire as discussed previously.)

The Condition of Other Banks in a Holding Company. Even if your bank is perfectly sound, it could become a "defined failure" if other banks or S&Ls owned by the same holding company are insolvent. This is what happened when all of the banks of the First Republic Bank system in Texas failed. Although many of the smaller First Republic banks were well capitalized and profitable, the FDIC required each of them to guarantee a one billion dollar loan it made to the troubled two lead banks of the holding company. When the lead banks defaulted, the FDIC also moved against the smaller banks, for whom one billion dollars was hopelessly out of reach. This maneuver netted the FDIC several good banks whose sale helped to defray its expenses in the resolution of the First Republic case.

Risks to Borrowers

"I have no money in that bank; my only connection with it is a loan. If the bank fails, the loan will not be my problem." Unfortunately, many people have already found out that this assumption is false. Many loans have "call-in" provisions. Loans known as "demand notes," "thirty day notes" and "ninety day notes," as well as certain other kinds of credit, can be recalled by the bank simply notifying the borrower that it does not intend to renew or "roll over" the loan. Some automobile loans and most unsecured business loans are of this type. When repayment is not forthcoming after the loan is "called in," collection measures and legal actions usually follow. If the FDIC or a similar agency is acting as the collection agent for a failed bank, it calls in as many loans as possible to speed along the liquidation process. Needless to say, if alternative sources of financing cannot be found quickly, personal bankruptcy can result. Many business owners, especially in Texas, have found this out the hard way.

Credit lines can be frozen at the amount currently outstanding. While such an action can put a seasonal firm out of business by denying borrowing at a critical time, individual consumers can be seriously affected as well. If you are using a high credit card limit or home equity line of credit to finance a college education, a home construction program or to tide your family over during unemployment, a frozen credit line can be an unwelcome jolt indeed. If payouts by the bank are stopped at a particularly inopportune time, financial disaster may result.

You should also check your loan documents for a provision that enables the bank to cancel your credit line if the bank is seized by a federal agency or is called upon by its regulators to reduce lending. For example, Empire of America, an insolvent thrift taken over in early 1990, had such a provision in some of its home equity line of credit agreements. The lesson should be clear. Read, understand thoroughly and be prepared to live with any call in or cancellation provisions in the loan contract. An example, taken from the Empire of America loan agreement, is illustrative.

> We can refuse to make additional extensions of credit or reduce your credit limit if . . . a regulatory agency has notified us that continued advances would constitute an unsafe and unsound business practice.

Special Risks to Business Customers

Because of large obligations such as payrolls, businesses typically face all of the risks that large depositors (over $100,000) encounter. However, commercial firms

58

can experience additional hazards too. Two of these are outlined below.

Loans and Deposits May Not Net Against Each Other. Often, as part of its lending provisions, a bank will require a firm to keep "compensating balances" on deposit. As stated earlier, if the bank is liquidated, the deposit balances may not be used to offset the loan amounts if the corporate identity of the entity holding the loan note differs from the entity at which the deposits are placed. For example, loans secured by real estate are often held by a mortgage subsidiary of a bank. Your deposit exposure must be analyzed in accordance with the amount you have borrowed from the exact same institution.

Lockboxes. Many business firms accelerate their cash flow by having clients send payments directly to the bank's post office box. The bank, immediately upon receiving the payments, credits the firm's account. This arrangement, called a lockbox, can cause considerable problems if the bank fails or closes the box abruptly. The rule of thumb is that it takes customers about six months to respond reliably to a change of address for payables. Meanwhile, the reduction in cash flow and the process of pursuing collection on large numbers of good accounts can be exceedingly costly.

General Liabilities of the Bank. Outside contractors and suppliers used by a bank sometimes mistake the $100,000 government deposit insurance as a blanket guarantee that covers any transaction with the bank. Needless to say, this assumption has no basis in reality. Obligations that a financial institution incurs in the normal course of doing business appear as liabilities (more precisely, non-deposit liabilities) on its balance sheet. If the institution is liquidated, its non-deposit liabilities are paid only after all of its deposit liabilities are satisfied. These deposit liabilities include reimbursement to the FDIC for any payouts they have made. Thus, when an institution is taken over to be liquidated by the regulators, there is little likelihood that any money will be left to pay bills from suppliers or contractors.

Risks to Investors

The term "investor" covers a broad class of individuals and business entities that put money into an institution in some form other then deposits. In other words, anyone whose stake is not protected by the $100,000 federal deposit insurance is an investor. This includes purchasers of stock or other securities of a bank, owners, partial owners and creditors. All have an interest in the institution's continuing good health.

Bank investors who are at the greatest risk are those who are uneducated about the health and operating procedures of their institutions. Since few recovery mechanisms benefit investors once severe problems set in, a bank investor must have one hundred percent foresight. Therefore, most serious bank owners and stockholders spend a significant amount of time and effort to understand the financial operations of their institution. If you have invested or are thinking of investing in a bank, be sure to heed the following rules of thumb.

Do not buy bank stock to "put away in a safe deposit box" in hope that someday, over the long term, it will be worth a great deal. The industry is changing too rapidly. Stock holdings in problem institutions should be unloaded while they still have value; appreciated stock in candidates for takeover (or that just have been taken over) has likely seen its major run up in value and should be sold. Of course, each individual case has its own special considerations, but the general rule is to have a plan or strategy, and follow your investment closely.

The principle of committing no more than you can afford to lose is especially pertinent when investing in banking institutions, particularly if you are more than a passive equity holder. In certain situations, an investment can carry an obligation that goes beyond the money originally invested. In some instances that obligation can be open-ended and disastrous. Becoming a principal equity holder in a firm that has taken title to land polluted with toxic waste can put you in a "deep pockets" position as far as many state and federal cleanup agencies are concerned. Investigate the details of your investment before committing. During the last few years, some of the nation's largest banks took over institutions in the Southwest without looking hard enough. Then they had to follow up their initial investment with considerably more money when bad loans in their new subsidiaries turned out to be worse than expected. The term "black hole" has been used to characterize an investment that is so bad, it sucks up all of the money an investor has.

Despite the risks inherent in the currently volatile banking industry, there are a number of generally unrecognized opportunities for investors who would consider buying into "top of the heap" institutions, particularly S&Ls. These are described further in Chapter 6.

A final word of caution to investors who are also managers or employees of the institutions in which they have ownership: Special care must be taken to avoid conflict, or appearances of conflict, with government norms regarding insider trading and fiducial responsibility.

Special Risks to Bank Officers and Management Personnel

Bankers have always had to be careful to avoid even the appearance of dishonesty. However, until recently, only the worst malfeasance brought penalties more severe than job loss. In a curious blend of frustration and vindictiveness, lawmakers have passed a number of draconian measures that make it possible for honest mistakes, or even an uncooperative attitude, to land a banker in prison.

Insider trading has received the most publicity. If a strong circumstantial case can be made that a bank employee has reduced his or her uninsured holdings on the strength of nonpublic knowledge about troubles developing at the institution, both civil and criminal sanctions can be brought against that employee.

More threatening, however, is the 1989 thrift bailout legislation, which gives regulators a large set of additional "tools" to use against officers and managers at failed institutions. It defines a broad array of banking crimes including misapplication of funds, incorrect entries on forms and false or misleading statements to government officials. Banking crimes now carry penalties of twenty years, and forfeiture of personal assets is also applicable in most cases. Civil penalties (no prison terms but fines from $25,000 to $1 million per day per infraction) apply to activities such as breach of fiduciary duty, unsafe and unsound banking practices, or reckless disregard for wrongful activity occurring at the bank. The standard of judgment appears to be: if the bank loses money, and it can be pinned upon a bank officer's act or omission, that person can be forced to make restitution from his or her own funds. Resigning one's job at a bank offers no protection. The law specifically empowers enforcement against employees who leave an institution before an investigation is launched.

Prosecutors are increasingly applying the harsh RICO (Racketeer Influenced and Corrupt Organizations) law sanctions against bank officers. The RICO law, supposedly intended for mobsters, allows most personal assets to be frozen before trial. As a result, it can be impossible for defendants to hire an effective legal representative. The near impossibility of defending against a RICO indictment almost always leads to plea bargains. Wall Street professionals widely believe that this was the threat that led Drexel Burnham Lambert to face near-certain bankruptcy by settling charges brought against it by the government.

Officers at insolvent S&Ls awaiting takeover are particularly vulnerable. Some lawyers recommend that bankers in this situation begin documenting justification for all transactions in which they have been involved. These bankers should emphasize responsible handling of situations that ultimately worked out unfavorably for the institution. As the 1990s unfold, it may well turn out that employees are the people who have to be most knowledgeable about the financial health of their bank.

Other Risks

Risks of Dealing with Non–Federally Insured Institutions. Unless an institution displays one of the *Federal* Deposit Insurance Fund emblems, its deposit insurance coverage is most likely lacking or limited. The only federal deposit insurances are the FDIC's BIF (Bank Insurance Fund) and SAIF (Savings Association Insurance Fund). For credit unions, the applicable federal deposit insurance is NCUSIF (National Credit Union Share Insurance Fund).

One less-known risk associated with non–federally insured institutions is the possibility that a bankruptcy court order will require you to reinstate funds that you had previously removed. Since financial data for uninsured institutions is often not publicly available, a court may hold that someone who flees from the bank did so on the basis of ''restricted information.'' This occurred in the case of an institution owned by fallen Tennessee bank magnate C. H. Butcher. Hundreds of depositors at his uninsured Southern Industrial Bank in Knoxville, who saw the storm brewing, withdrew their money several months before the institution closed in 1983. In 1987, a judge ordered them to turn over those funds to the bankruptcy court for distribution to creditors whose claims had higher legal priority in the liquidation proceedings! In short, they lost their money four years after the bank closed!

Institutions Under Government Control. Currently, hundreds of insolvent financial institutions are being operated by government agencies, pending their liquidation. The term "conservatorship," which applies to this situation, sounds pleasant enough, but the harsh reality is that these are failed institutions that concentrate as much risk as exists anywhere in the federally insured banking system. Most of these insolvent institutions are savings and loan associations that have been taken over by the Resolution Trust Corporation (RTC). Despite the fact that this part of the banking industry is nationalized, i.e., is an arm of the U.S. government, the institutions are still, for the most part, being operated individually, under their original charters. The facade, that the institution is continuing as a private corporate entity with a government administrator running it, is often maintained for the government's convenience. Herein lies a potential trap, since government "takeover" of the management of an institution is very distinct from liquidation or bankruptcy proceedings. In bankruptcy, a court can offer its guarantee that new obligations of the institution will be honored. If there are no bankruptcy proceedings, the protection a court provides to new creditors is not available. All that is available is the administrator's word.

The possibility is that while an insolvent institution under government control continues in business, it may build up significant non-deposit liabilities such as unpaid bills to suppliers. If the creditors have contracted with the institution (instead of with the government), the institution's obligations to them may be wiped out when the institution is finally sold or liquidated. As of this writing, there have been no reports of federal bank liquidators converting deposit liabilities into non-deposit liabilities in this manner. However, as pressure increases on the government to come up with hundreds of billions of dollars in bailout money, it will be sure to explore other legal ways of reaching into vulnerable pockets. Anyone dealing with an insolvent S&L should be exceptionally cautious, especially if that thrift is being operated by a U.S. government agency. When conducting transactions with government-run insolvent institutions, you need to be particularly aware of the following factors.

- If payments to you for products or services rendered are guaranteed by the institution alone, and not by the government, you have a significant risk of not being paid.
- When you enter into a contract that the insolvent institution decides later to back away from, ordinary civil and legal remedies can be useless. Even if you "win" a judgment, when the institution is liquidated, there will be no money to pay any awards. In effect, an insolvent institution is "judgment proof."
- If you are purchasing property from a government-controlled institution, any funds you commit to the deal prior to your receipt of a clear title are at risk. Similarly, any vulnerability you have to delays in completion of the deal (e.g., if being "slow rolled" could cause you to suffer losses or limit your ability to follow through) must be recognized for the additional risk it adds.
- An unfamiliarity with the fine details of how the government does business, particularly contract business, can cause you to underestimate both the cost of complying with governmental legalisms and the cost of dealing with cash flow difficulties brought on by normal bureaucratic routine (e.g.,

delays and the large number of approvals required for each stage of a deal's progress).

- In any disagreement or misunderstanding with the administrators of an institution under government control, your opponent will be able to draw upon a wide array of government resources to confront you. Even if you could otherwise prevail, the doctrine of sovereign immunity (you cannot sue the government or any of its agencies unless you are granted special permission) can always be invoked to hold you at bay.

- The government can renege on any commitments before a deal is completed, or it can unwind a deal after the fact. The disturbing trend toward this kind of behavior by Uncle Sam is discussed below.

The Government's Increasing Duplicity

While our government's power to regulate the financial environment is nearly total, its elected officials have usually pursued policies that adhere to past agreements and avoid "after the fact" legislative changes—retroactive laws designed to strip citizens of lawful rights or gains. Until recently legislators adhered to the principle set forth by the nation's founders in the constitutional statement, "Congress shall pass no ex post facto law."

The following examples offer evidence of the government's increasing abuse of isolated economic targets that possess little political clout, but have sizable exposed resources.

- Income tax law revisions in 1986 changed capital gains and passive income rules on assets *already acquired*. This pulled the financial rug out from under many investors who had locked themselves

66

into long-term commitments under the previous, more favorable rules. Several analysts point to this action, and the uncertainty it created, as a significant cause of the current real estate downturn (and the resulting problems it has created for banks and thrifts).

- In the early and mid 1980s, one approach used by federal regulators for disposing of insolvent S&Ls cheaply was to encourage nearby healthier institutions to absorb the problem institutions into their organizations. To turn such an otherwise silly financial transaction into an attractive one, the acquiring S&L was given thirty years to fully reflect the insolvent S&L's accumulated losses on its balance sheet. This "goodwill" provision kept the acquiring S&L from being financially penalized, unless it could not turn its acquisition around in roughly the length of time required for all of the mortgages on the insolvent institution's books to mature. However, after less than ten years, Congress abruptly ended this arrangement. Now many S&Ls that played to the government's tune are being pressed to come up with money (capital) to make up for leftover losses from their previous acquisitions. Some, in fact, have themselves been declared insolvent and have been taken over by federal regulators.

- Between seventy and eighty private investors allowed themselves to be convinced, in 1988, that it was worth their while to take failed S&Ls off the government's hands. The deals were done hurriedly by regulators in an effort to stop the financial hemorrhaging of billions of dollars from many of these institutions. Amid an atmosphere of considerable uncertainty and risk, these investors took on the responsibilities of ownership in return for a variety of inducements from our money-short government. Some of these inducements stemmed from favorable tax laws then in effect; other inducements were periodic payments by the government to help in managing problem properties and government money to offset some of the losses on bad loans held by the S&L being sold. Nonetheless, the risks were severe enough that several of the institutions created by these deals have already failed. Yet, in 1990, the Resolution Trust Corporation is conducting congressionally mandated "studies" of these transactions. The purpose of the studies is to recommend which provisions of the successful transactions should be revoked.

- In some of the 1988 S&L sales, the government granted the acquirers relief from meeting the full measure of capital required of most S&Ls. This forbearance was negotiated to extend for a certain number of years in each case, generating savings for the new management to make up for the government's lack of funds to put into each deal. In 1990, the Office of Thrift Supervision announced that many of these provisions would become "inoperative" or would be "phased out."

- Strong-arm tactics of a different sort were described earlier in this chapter in the story about the former First Republic Holding Company of Texas. The FDIC insisted that the company's one-billion-dollar bailout loan be guaranteed by all eighty-one banks in the holding company. Many of these institutions, with total assets well under $100 million, had no way to guarantee such a note, and when First Republic's lead banks later defaulted on the loan, the impossible obligation that had been levied on the small banks was used by the FDIC as an excuse to declare them insolvent. While this worked to the government's advantage, many Texas families who had owned these well-run banks for generations before joining one of First Republic's forerunner holding companies, suffered serious financial losses or ruin.

- In the area of federal deposit insurance, several changes are being "phased in" to equalize provisions of the bank and S&L coverages for accounts over $100,000. Needless to say, these clauses do not increase coverage. The problem is that no regard is being given to account holders that are unable to respond to the changes without incurring serious penalties.

- Presently, the FDIC intends to revise coverage on certain types of pension plans ("457 plans") to $100,000 per plan as opposed to the current $100,000 multiplied by the number of plan members. Since many pensioners and future pensioners are locked into their plans by their employers' rules, or by the tax code, these people's retirement funds will soon be threatened by the specter of bank failures.

Will the government continue to renege on past agreements and make new rules that trap citizens in the provisions of earlier legislation? Will the nibbling away at the edges of the deposit insurance coverage get worse? As of this writing there has been little political protest about the examples cited above. On the other hand, the government's financial difficulties in dealing with the banking crisis continue to snowball. This trend definitely favors the view that Uncle Sam's hand will have less and less regard for contractual niceties, commitments or traditional views of fair dealing.

What additional risks does this disturbing trend levy on those who deal with banks, S&Ls and credit unions? While it is impossible to assess with any degree of confidence the downside effects of evolving government policies, four courses of action seem prudent:

1. Know your bank and its holding company, as well as other financial institutions with which you deal. Are they healthy, or not?
2. Conduct your banking with strong institutions when possible.
3. Understand fully all of your banking transactions and the kinds of accounts you use.
4. Try to arrange your banking affairs so that you are not critically dependent upon the government living up to all of its promises.

5

THE SAFEST BANKS AND HOW TO CHOOSE THEM

During the three decades that followed World War Two, banking safety was a nonissue, and it was taken for granted that banks and bankers were an unchanging (if somewhat uninteresting) part of the nation's financial scene. Once your banker got to know you and your reputation for careful money management, he would be there to finance that new car, the house, the small business venture or a college education.

While there is no returning to that more pleasant banking era, it is still possible to identify institutions that are not seeking rapid growth, that operate very conservatively and that are clearly in banking for the long haul. These bankers may not be the most imaginative businessmen in the world, or the most generous, but they are the appropriate people with whom to build long-term financial relationships. As one client of such a bank was heard to exclaim, "I am not surprised they are in such good shape; they are so cheap they do not even give out calendars at Christmastime!"

In addition to the safety considerations discussed in earlier chapters, an institution which is likely to stay put for many years offers a number of advantages to consumers.

For example, when the people at a bank learn who you are and about your, hopefully responsible, financial habits, you can expect near-automatic approval of reasonable loan requests, an occasional favor (such as accommodating a large deposit five minutes after closing at the beginning of a long weekend) and the privilege of bypassing the petty identification procedures required at institutions where you are unrecognized.

Common Characteristics That Strong Banks Share

Conservatively operated banks are managed by people who avoid risk. They are low rollers who are content to earn their living from the myriad of ''percentage plays'' that comprise the traditional banking business. A number of common attributes characterize such institutions. They are listed below.

- Capital: plenty of it
- Loans: a minimum number of problems
- Profitability: always profitable, quarter after quarter, year after year
- Size: large enough not to be one-room operations yet not so large as to run at bare minimum capital levels
- Stability: no appreciable growth or shrinkage throughout the year
- Liquidity: plenty of funds on hand to pay bills and handle occasional withdrawals
- Diversity: loan portfolios avoid undue concentration in one lending area, or to just a few borrowers
- Deposit base: no undue reliance on brokered, out-of-country or uninsured deposits

Note that banks that are this conservative are not necessarily good investment opportunities. Returns to shareholders are generally secondary to the type of stability and conservative policies these institutions follow. The possible exception is the small, well-run institution that could be a candidate for buyout by a larger bank.

What Are the Safety Advantages of a Larger Bank?

Most people believe that larger banks are less likely to fail than smaller ones. This may be because, prior to 1980, most bank failures were small institutions. However, during the last decade, even though many more small banks failed than did large ones, the uneven proportion of small banks to large banks easily accounted for the difference. Nonetheless, it is still commonly held that large banks are more safe. A plausible rationale could be based on the protection that size offers. A large institution is better situated to suffer occasional loan losses simply because it can absorb more "hits" than can a small institution. For example, a million-dollar bounced check sank the Bank of Hohenwald (Tennessee) in 1982. Such an occurrence would likely have caused no more than the loss of several jobs at a much larger institution.

In practice, medium-sized and larger banks have as many, or more, problems as small institutions. (The very largest banks are special; they are discussed separately below.) One of the reasons is that smaller banks are typically required to own a greater portion of their assets (i.e., to possess more capital) than are larger institutions. Some analysts believe that, with more of their own money at stake, managements at smaller institutions naturally tend to be more conservative. Overall, our studies have shown

73

that there is no strong trend either way. Factors other than size are more important in evaluating bank safety.

Are Some Banks Too Big to Fail?

Many people assume that the FDIC does not dare allow a megabank to fail for fear of the damage it could cause the economy. This is known as the "too big to fail" doctrine. The doctrine was well articulated by the Continental Illinois bailout in 1984. At that time, two groups within the FDIC encouraged different policies. One group favored letting the bank fail and selling or liquidating it as had been done with most other bank failures that had occurred up to then. The other argued that the risk to the economy was too great a chance to take—better to fire the bank's management and wipe out the stockholders (as in any other bank failure) but guarantee that uninsured depositors and creditors would not lose their money. Considerable debate followed, with group one arguing that once the government established the precedent by bailing out depositors at Continental, future regulators would dare not break it when the next large bank got into trouble. Worse yet, they argued, the commercial community would recognize the regulators' softness toward large institutions and would move their business to the top banks, regardless of how shaky they might be. This behavior, of course, is exactly what the regulatory agencies want to discourage.

As history shows, group two won the argument and Continental Bank was "saved." As group one predicted, each time another troubled large bank came up as a potential failure candidate, the FDIC backed down. This de facto policy persists today. However, several forces are at work which may cause it to change. They are:

- The FDIC has received considerable criticism from Congress for treating large banks and exceedingly wealthy depositors differently from small banks and depositors modestly over the $100,000 insurance limit.

- The cost to the Bank Insurance Fund in a large bank bailout can easily run close to $4 billion or more. (Some of this money, as in the case of Continental Illinois, may be recovered after several years.) Even if the FDIC is able to treat such an amount as a loan until the bailed institution gets back on its feet, part of its $14 billion insurance fund becomes tied up and unavailable to pay depositors, if needed. Only a few such bailouts, back to back, would wipe out all of the Bank Insurance Fund. Needless to say, the bank regulators do not relish replaying the S&L crisis in their own backyard. As a result, each "too big to fail" case is argued furiously among federal banking agency policy makers.

- Recently, group one has advocated allowing a carefully selected large bank to go into liquidation. Their idea is to choose an institution where there is minimal potential for serious economic dislocation. This action, they argue, will send a message to the financial community that the theory that a bank is "too big to fail" is too unpredictable to rely upon.

How large does an institution have to become before it passes the threshold that makes it too big to fail? Continental Illinois had $39 billion in assets. First City of Texas, with $9.8 billion and 60 banks, was also bailed out. So was First Republic, also in Texas, which possessed $36.4 billion and 81 banks. Does Bank of New England, starting with $34 billion and 9 banks as it faces the regulators, also qualify? As of this writing, only the future will tell.

Banks That Have Demonstrated
Staying Power

In the early 1980s, VERIBANC conducted a wide-ranging study of all of the banks and S&Ls that had failed and, to the extent we could determine, the reasons why. For example, up to that time, with only a few exceptions, all of the failures had been smaller than $50 million. We also considered additional factors that we believed could cause future failures. This study resulted in the list of criteria and specifications for safe banks listed below. Banks that meet these criteria are given the name "Blue Ribbon Banks" and reports listing them (Blue Bank Reports) have been published since 1982.

The distinguishing feature of Blue Ribbon Banks is that, despite the three- to four-month delay in availability of bank financial data used to perform the evaluations, no bank that has met the Blue Ribbon Bank criteria has ever failed. That certainly is not to say that the approximately 1,000 to 1,300 banks that satisfy these stringent specifications each quarter are the nation's only safe banks. Far from it. Many banks that do not meet all of the criteria listed below are exceedingly sound. However, the Blue Ribbon Banks are so conservatively run that they may be thought of as having an extra, probably unnecessary margin of caution.

Criteria Used to Select Blue Ribbon Banks

All of the following conditions must be satisfied for a bank to be classified in the Blue Ribbon category described above. The first three criteria must be met in each of the two latest financial quarters.

* Total assets must exceed $50 million.
* Equity must exceed 7.5 percent of assets.
* Net income after extraordinary items and taxes must be positive (i.e., the bank must be profitable).

The following criteria must be met in the most recent financial quarter.

* Liquid assets (assets readily convertible to cash within a year) must be at least 45 percent of total deposits.
* Equity, discounted for problem loans in excess of loan loss reserves, must exceed 6 percent of assets.
* Total overseas lending must not exceed the bank's equity.
* The equity of the bank (dollar amount) must not have declined from its value in the previous quarter.
* Its liquidity (liquid assets divided by deposits) must not have increased by more than 50 percent or decreased by more than 33 percent since the previous quarter.

If the bank is owned by a holding company, any other bank that belongs to the same holding company owner (even if ownership is through a different subsidiary holding company) must meet both of the following conditions for the latest quarter.

- Equity must exceed 3 percent of assets.
- If the bank suffered net losses during the quarter, those losses must amount to less than 18.75 percent of its end-of-quarter equity.

"Trigger conditions" apply when a bank satisfies all of the criteria listed previously, but reported asset, equity or net income changes in excess of 10 percent from the previous quarter's value. In those instances, the following additional criteria must be met.

- Net income rate of return on assets must exceed median profitability for all banks in the most recent financial quarter.
- Demand deposits and short-term liabilities (payable in less than one year) must not have declined by more than 10 percent over the quarter.
- Brokered deposits must not exceed 10 percent of total deposits.
- Foreign deposits must not exceed 10 percent of total deposits.
- Insider lending must not exceed 10 percent of equity.
- Gross off–balance sheet commitments must not exceed total assets.
- Lending must not be highly concentrated in the major categories of agriculture, residential real estate, commercial real estate, commercial and industrial financing, personal lending, bankers acceptances and lease financing. Highly concentrated means more than twice the average percentage of total loans in any category. The average is

computed for all U.S. commercial banks and savings banks.

Selected Blue Ribbon Banks

Over one thousand banks nationwide meet the criteria described in the foregoing section. Although space precludes listing all of them, the following 324 institutions met the criteria for the quarter ending September 30, 1989, and each previous quarter, going back for two years. Thus, the banks listed below have a long-standing track record of very conservative management practice. The list is supplied, courtesy of VERIBANC, Inc., with the understanding that these banks should not necessarily be viewed as the best, the safest or the strongest institutions in the country or as the only institutions that meet high standards. It should also be recognized that the condition of these banks may change.

The Blue Ribbon Bank List

	Commercial Bank Name	City
ALABAMA	First National Bank of Atmore	Atmore
	Peoples Savings Bank	Clanton
	Robertson Banking Company	Demopolis
	Citizens Bank	Fayette
	First Bank of Fayette	Fayette
	First National Bank of Florence	Florence
	Citizens Bank of Hartselle	Hartselle

	Commercial Bank Name	**City**
ALABAMA (cont.)	Valley National Bank	Lanett
	Monroe County Bank	Monroeville
	Union Banking and Trust Company	Montgomery
	Union State Bank	Pell City
	Citizens Bank and Trust Company Savings Company	Russellville
	First National Bank	Scottsboro
	First National Bank of Talladega	Talladega
	Citizens Bank	Winfield
ALASKA	First National Bank of Anchorage	Anchorage
	First Bank	Ketchikan
ARKANSAS	Elk Horn Banking and Trust Company	Arkadelphia
	First National Bank of Berryville	Berryville
	First National Bank of Crossett	Crossett
	First National Bank of De Queen	De Queen
	First National Bank in Green Forest	Green Forest
	Farmers Bank	Greenwood
	First National Bank of Huntsville	Huntsville
	First National Bank and Trust Company of Mountain Home	Mountain Home
	First National Bank	Paragould
	First National Bank	Searcy
	First National Bank of Springdale	Springdale
	State First National Bank	Texarkana

	Commercial Bank Name	**City**
ARKANSAS (cont.)	First State Bank of Warren	Warren
	Bank of West Memphis	West Memphis
CALIFORNIA	Valley National Bank	Glendale
	Farmers and Merchants Bank of Long Beach	Long Beach
	Mechanics Bank of Richmond	Richmond
	Merchants National Bank	Sacramento
	First State Bank of the Oaks	Thousand Oaks
	Savings Bank of Mendocino City	Ukiah
COLORADO	Bank of Douglas County	Castle Rock
	Omnibank Southeast	Denver
	Farmers State Bank	Fort Morgan
CONNECTICUT	Citizens National Bank	Putnam
DISTRICT OF COLUMBIA	National Capital Bank of Washington	Washington
FLORIDA	First National Bank of Clearwater	Clearwater
	First National Bank of Crestview	Crestview
	Bank of Inverness	Inverness
	First Guaranty Banking and Trust Company	Jacksonville
	Key Biscayne Banking and Trust Company	Key Biscayne
	Florida Keys First State Bank	Key West
	Coconut Grove Bank	Miami

	Commercial Bank Name	*City*
FLORIDA (cont.)	Trade National Bank	Miami
	United National Bank of Miami	Miami
	Jefferson National Bank at Sunny Isles	North Miami Beach
GEORGIA	Granite City Bank	Elberton
	Bank of LaFayette	LaFayette
	Brand Banking Company	Lawrenceville
	Farmers and Merchants Bank	Summerville
	Bank of Upson	Thomaston
	Bank of Thomson	Thomson
	Citizens Bank of Toccoa	Toccoa
IDAHO	Bank of Commerce	Idaho Falls
ILLINOIS	Algonquin State Bank	Algonquin
	National Bank of Commerce	Berkeley
	First State Bank	Calumet City
	First National Bank in Carlyle	Carlyle
	National Bank of Carmi	Carmi
	Carrollton Banking and Trust Company	Carrollton
	Buena Vista National Bank of Chester	Chester
	District National Bank of Chicago	Chicago
	East Side Banking and Trust Company	Chicago
	Heritage Bank of Country Club Hills	Country Club Hills
	Home State Bank	Crystal Lake
	Soy Capital Banking and Trust Company	Decatur
	Dixon National Bank	Dixon
	First National Bank of Dwight	Dwight

	Commercial Bank Name	**City**
ILLINOIS (cont.)	Effingham State Bank	Effingham
	National Bank of Fairbury	Fairbury
	Farmers and Mechanics Bank	Galesburg
	Central Trust and Savings Bank	Geneseo
	Harrisburg National Bank	Harrisburg
	Havana National Bank	Havana
	Peoples Bank of Mary Crest	Kankakee
	First National Bank of Illinois	Lansing
	Citizens National Bank	Macomb
	Bank of Egypt	Marion
	First National Bank	McHenry
	National Bank of Mendota	Mendota
	City National Bank of Metropolis	Metropolis
	Blackhawk State Bank	Milan
	Peoples State Bank	Newton
	Bank of O'Fallon	O'Fallon
	First National Bank in Olney	Olney
	State Bank of Orion	Orion
	First National Bank of Pana	Pana
	Herget National Bank of Pekin	Pekin
	National Bank of Petersburg	Petersburg
	Pontiac National Bank	Pontiac
	Rock Island Bank	Rock Island
	First State Bank	Round Lake
	Farmers State Bank	Somonauk
	Spring Valley City Bank	Spring Valley
	Tuscola National Bank	Tuscola
	First National Bank of Waterloo	Waterloo
	Bank of West Frankfort	West Frankfort
INDIANA	First Bank of Berne	Berne
	Peoples Trust and Savings Bank	Boonville

Commercial Bank Name	City
INDIANA (cont.)	
Hendricks County Banking and Trust Company	Brownsburg
First Farmers National Bank	Converse
Fountain Trust Company	Covington
National City Bank of Evansville	Evansville
Greenfield Banking Company	Greenfield
State Bank of Lizton	Lizton
Citizens State Bank	New Castle
Orange County Bank	Paoli
Citizens National Bank of Tell City	Tell City
Merchants National Bank, Terre Haute	Terre Haute
Security Bank and Trust Company	Vincennes
American Trust and Savings Bank	Whiting
IOWA	
Brenton Banking and Trust Company	Adel
Iowa State Bank	Algona
First National Bank	Ames
Citizens Savings Bank	Anamosa
Farmers and Merchants Banking and Trust Company	Burlington
First Trust and Savings Bank	Cedar Rapids
Guaranty Bank and Trust Company	Cedar Rapids
Cherokee State Bank	Cherokee
Clear Lake Banking and Trust Company	Clear Lake
Clinton National Bank	Clinton
Iowa State Savings Bank	Clinton
Davenport Banking and Trust Company	Davenport

	Commercial Bank Name	**City**
IOWA (cont.)	Decorah State Bank	Decorah
	East Des Moines National Bank	Des Moines
	Liberty Trust and Savings Bank	Durant
	First National Bank of Hampton	Hampton
	Shelby County State Bank	Harlan
	Iowa Falls State Bank	Iowa Falls
	Le Mars Savings Bank	Le Mars
	Central State Bank	Muscatine
	Oelwein State Bank	Oelwein
	Home Trust and Savings Bank	Osage
	Osage Farmers National Bank	Osage
	South Ottumwa Savings Bank	Ottumwa
	Marion County State Bank	Pella
	Montgomery County National Bank, Red Oak	Red Oak
	State Bank of Toledo	Toledo
	State Bank of Waverly	Waverly
	First National Bank of West Union	West Union
KANSAS	Home National Bank of Arkansas City	Arkansas City
	Union State Bank	Clay Center
	Fidelity State Banking and Trust Company	Dodge City
	First National Bank of Hutchinson	Hutchinson
	Douglas County Bank	Lawrence
	Union National Bank and Trust Company of Manhattan	Manhattan
	City National Bank of Pittsburg	Pittsburg

	Commercial Bank Name	**City**
KENTUCKY	Bank of Ashland	Ashland
	Kentucky Farms Bank, Catlettsburg	Catlettsburg
	Farmers Banking and Trust Company Capital Trust Company	Frankfort
	Simpson County Bank	Franklin
	First National Bank of Manchester	Manchester
	First National Bank of Mayfield	Mayfield
	Bank of Maysville	Maysville
	Bank of Murray	Murray
	Peoples Bank of Murray	Murray
	Citizens National Bank of Russellville	Russellville
LOUISIANA	St. Bernard Banking and Trust Company	Arabi
	First National Bank in De Ridder	De Ridder
	Tri Parish Banking and Trust Company	Eunice
	Metairie Banking and Trust Company	Metairie
	Southern National Bank at Tallulah	Tallulah
	First American Banking and Trust Company	Vacherie
MARYLAND	Carrollton Bank of Baltimore	Baltimore
	Elkridge National Bank	Elkridge
MICHIGAN	Chelsea State Bank	Chelsea
	Chemical Bank, Clare	Clare
	Hastings City Bank	Hastings
	First National Bank, Iron Mountain	Iron Mountain

	Commercial Bank Name	*City*
MICHIGAN (cont.)	City Banking and Trust Company	Jackson
	Chemical Banking and Trust Company	Midland
	Warren Bank	Warren
MINNESOTA	Buffalo National Bank	Buffalo
	Golden Valley Bank: A United Bank	Golden Valley
	Grand Rapids State Bank	Grand Rapids
	First National Bank of St. Peter	St. Peter
	Northern State Bank of Thief River Falls	Thief River Falls
	Winona National and Savings Bank	Winona
MISSISSIPPI	Peoples Bank of Delta	Indianola
	First National Bank of Pontotoc	Pontotoc
	Peoples Bank	Ripley
MISSOURI	First National Bank of Gallatin	Gallatin
	Hannibal National Bank	Hannibal
	Exchange National Bank of Jefferson City	Jefferson City
	Lemay Banking and Trust Company	Lemay
	Mercantile Bank	Louisiana
	Bank of Odessa	Odessa
	First National Bank of Sikeston	Sikeston
	Bremen Banking and Trust Company	St. Louis
	Trenton Trust Company	Trenton
	West Plains Bank	West Plains

	Commercial Bank Name	**City**
MONTANA	Farmers State Bank	Conrad
	Yellowstone Bank	Laurel
NEBRASKA	First National Bank and Trust Company	Falls City
	Geneva State Bank	Geneva
	O'Neill National Bank	O'Neill
	Scotts Bluff National Bank and Trust Company	Scotts Bluff
	Jones National Bank and Trust Company, Seward	Seward
	First National Bank of Valentine	Valentine
NEW JERSEY	United Counties Trust Company	Cranford
	Newton Trust Company	Newton
NEW YORK	Alden State Bank	Alden
	Evans National Bank of Angola	Angola
	Putnam County National Bank of Carmel	Carmel
	National Bank of Coxsackie	Coxsackie
	First National Bank of Long Island	Glen Head
	City National Bank and Trust Company	Gloversville
	Mahopac National Bank	Mahopac
	Orange County Trust Company	Middletown
	Fiduciary Trust Company	New York
	Merchants Bank of New York	New York
	Tioga State Bank	Spencer
	Bank of Utica	Utica
	National Bank of Delaware County, Walton	Walton

	Commercial Bank Name	City
NORTH CAROLINA	Republic Banking and Trust Company	Charlotte
	Fidelity Bank	Fuquay-Varina
	Security Banking and Trust Company	Salisbury
	First National Bank of Shelby	Shelby
OHIO	First National Bank, Barnesville	Barnesville
	Citizens Savings Bank	Martins Ferry
	Middlefield Banking Company	Middlefield
	First National Bank	Orrville
	Citizens Banking Company	Sandusky
	Security National Bank and Trust Company	Springfield
	Miners and Mechanics Savings and Trust Company	Steubenville
	First National Bank of Waverly	Waverly
OKLAHOMA	Oklahoma State Bank	Ada
	First National Bank of Altus	Altus
	Rogers County Bank	Claremore
	First National Bank and Trust Company	McAlester
	First National Bank of Pauls Valley	Pauls Valley
OREGON	National Security Bank	Newport
	Pioneer Trust Bank	Salem
PENNSYLVANIA	Apollo Trust Company	Apollo
	Merchants National Bank of Bangor	Bangor
	County National Bank	Clearfield

	Commercial Bank Name	*City*
PENNSYLVANIA (cont.)	Denver National Bank	Denver
	Fidelity Deposits and Discounts	Dunmore
	Ephrata National Bank	Ephrata
	First National Bank in Fleetwood	Fleetwood
	Farmers and Merchants Bank	Honesdale
	Jonestown Bank and Trust Company	Jonestown
	Commercial National Bank, Westmoreland	Latrobe
	Second National Bank of Masontown	Masontown
	Mid Penn Bank	Millersburg
	Iron and Glass Bank	Pittsburgh
	Peoples Bank of Unity	Plum Boro
	Citizens and Northern Bank	Ralston
	Penn Security Banking and Trust Company	Scranton
SOUTH CAROLINA	First National Bank of Pickens County	Easley
	Enterprise Bank of South Carolina	Ehrhardt
SOUTH DAKOTA	Pioneer Banking and Trust Company	Belle Fourche
	Dakota State Bank	Milbank
	Valley National Bank	Sioux Falls
TENNESSEE	Citizens National Bank of Athens	Athens
	Barretville Banking and Trust Company	Barretville
	Bank of Dickson	Dickson
	Greene County Bank	Greeneville
	Peoples National Bank, La Follette	La Follette

	Commercial Bank Name	**City**
TENNESSEE (cont.)	First National Bank of Lawrenceburg	Lawrenceburg
	Peoples and Union Bank	Lewisburg
	Bank of Madisonville	Madisonville
	City Banking and Trust Company	McMinnville
	Union Bank	Pulaski
	Citizens Banking and Trust Company of Grainger	Rutledge
TEXAS	First National Bank of Athens	Athens
	First National Bank of Bay City	Bay City
	First National Bank in Big Spring	Big Spring
	Citizens National Bank of Cameron	Cameron
	First State Banking and Trust Company	Carthage
	First State Bank	Columbus
	Comanche National Bank	Comanche
	Citizens State Bank	Giddings
	First Banking and Trust Company	Groves
	Border Bank	Hidalgo
	Citizens National Bank of Hillsboro	Hillsboro
	First National Bank	Jasper
	Kermit State Bank	Kermit
	First National Bank	Killeen
	First Lockhart National Bank	Lockhart
	Liberty State Bank	Lubbock
	Ozona National Bank	Ozona
	Citizens Bank	Rusk
	Seguin State Banking and Trust Company	Seguin
	First State Bank	Spearman

	Commercial Bank Name	**City**
TEXAS (cont.)	American National Bank Yoakum National Bank	Texarkana Yoakum
UTAH	Barnes Banking Company	Kaysville
VIRGINIA	First National Bank of Clifton Forge	Clifton Forge
WASHINGTON	Skagit State Bank	Burlington
WEST VIRGINIA	Community Banking and Trust Company of Harrison County	Clarksburg
	Davis Trust Company	Elkins
	First National Bank of Hinton	Hinton
	National Bank of Summers	Hinton
	Albright National Bank of Kingwood	Kingwood
	Bank of Man	Man
	Peoples Bank of Mullens	Mullens
	Potomac Valley Bank	Petersburg
	National Bank Commerce	South Charleston
	Home National Bank of Sutton	Sutton
	Bank of Weirton	Weirton
	Citizens Bank	Weston
	First National Bank and Trust Company of Wheeling	Wheeling
	Security National Bank and Trust Company	Wheeling
	Wheeling Dollar Bank	Wheeling
	First National Bank of Williamson	Williamson
WISCONSIN	Boscobel State Bank Northwestern Bank	Boscobel Chippewa Falls

	Commercial Bank Name	*City*
WISCONSIN (cont.)	First American Banking and Trust Company	Fort Atkinson
	Kilbourn State Bank	Milwaukee
	Port Washington State Bank	Port Washington
	Peoples State Bank	Prairie du Chien
	Bank of Prairie Du Sac	Prairie du Sac
	Pulaski State Bank	Pulaski
	M&I First National Bank	West Bend
WYOMING	Key Bank of Wyoming	Kemmerer
	North Side State Bank	Rock Springs
	Rock Springs National Bank	Rock Springs

6

OPPORTUNITIES IN BANKING AND NEW RELATIONSHIPS BETWEEN BANKING AND REAL ESTATE

Up until a few years ago, banking was a placid, almost risk-free business consisting of little more than the various "percentage games" associated with borrowing and lending money and other related services. Now, as great institutions and whole industries stumble, as hundreds of billions of dollars of business is being redistributed, and as problems multiply, a whole array of opportunities are available to the creative, the enterprising and those who are simply clever. Interesting, challenging and rewarding careers that were unimaginable a few years ago now beckon to those looking to make their efforts felt. Many will get rich in the process. This chapter provides a quick look at some of these opportunities and a glimpse of the silver lining within the cloud of the banking crisis.

Investment in the Banking Industry

Because of the banking crisis, investment opportunities abound. From purchases of good, well-run, undervalued institutions' stock to starting a new bank (our regulatory environment encourages startups); carefully selected banking investments may provide the best opportunity of the century. Bank customers, reeling in the face of uncertainty, failures, takeovers and the mass marketing policies of many institutions, are realigning their loyalties. A host of "special niches" exist, waiting for alert firms to exploit them. Current weaknesses include assessing borrower credit quality, providing more convenient and rapid service, offering loan products more tuned to the tax laws (like the very successful home equity lines of credit) and more. Investors who can tap into these niches (or tap into the institutions that do) should be rewarded amply.

Well-run S&Ls are a special opportunity. Tarred with the brush of the ongoing federal bailout of insolvents and bedeviled by a suddenly oppressive regulatory environment, many managements would welcome the chance to sell out, to bring in new blood or to share the load.

On the other hand, as of this writing, the insolvent thrifts being "warehoused" by the government (in the Resolution Trust Corporation's conservatorship program) appear to be uninviting investments. They are often encumbered by red tape, beset with problems that are difficult to measure, and deprived by the departure of their best talent. Frank Gentry of NCNB, an acquisition-minded bank, observes that "the longer a thrift is in [federal] conservatorship, the more likely its better employees will have left." As a result, most investors have been staying away from Uncle Sam's inventory and the threat of vilification (for profiting at the taxpayers' expense) that could follow a deal that works out well.

Indications are that this stalemate may end. Already there is talk in Washington about "more realism" being needed to speed disposal of failed thrifts. Such a change is imperative if the thrift crisis is to be solved.

A summary of factors that are currently favorable to would-be bank investors is presented on the facing page.

- General disfavor with which the investment community now views bank and thrift stocks (and reflection of that disfavor in current low stock prices).
- Continuing pressure on strong, well-capitalized institutions (particularly S&Ls) to sell out to larger acquirers.
- Particular needs by many well-managed and profitable S&Ls to raise capital to meet (or stay ahead of) regulatory requirements that will be tightening over the next several years.
- Availability of far more detailed financial operating data about federally insured banks and thrifts than is obtainable for most other kinds of corporations (and the unawareness by most investors of the degree of detail that can be accessed).
- The capability of financial research organizations to conduct data base searches for candidate banking institutions meeting a financial profile that suits a particular investment or acquisition strategy. Many investors also work from in-house data bases to develop lists of prospect banks.

Real Estate: New Thinking Needed

Some of the greatest changes in the banking industry are driven by and, in turn, are influencing purchases and sales of property. The traditional view about real estate investment has been "people multiply but land does not. Therefore, over the long term, demand for property must increase and values have to appreciate." While this may be true in the very long run, many experts believe that the next several years (or more) will be a time of correction in most of the country. Real estate values are expected to slowly drift downward toward an equilibrium in which the

97

after-tax return on owned property will approach more closely the return provided by other reasonably safe investments. The experts also believe that residential property prices will remain at or below current levels until the median price of homes is more within the reach of middle-income working couples.

Reasons for this reversal include the recent excessive running up of real estate prices in many parts of the country, tax law changes discouraging investment property ownership, cooling of the economy, and additional ownership liability risk (toxic wastes, radon, lead paint, environmental hazards, tenant activism, rent control, etc.). On top of these factors is a huge, nationwide glut of foreclosed properties, owned by the government's Resolution Trust Corporation, and the large numbers of sale-prone property owners who are in financial trouble. This latter fact is more serious than is widely recognized. For example, according to third and fourth quarter 1989 data analyzed at VERIBANC, 7 percent of all property in the country had owners who were delinquent on their mortgages or had already suffered foreclosure. Clearly, there is a need for investors—"slow buck artists"—who understand these new dynamics and have the staying power to await the next real estate boom. Opportunity abounds for new types of deal facilitators who can tune into down markets—appraisers, auctioneers, brokers, financiers, interim managers, and workout specialists.

Troubled Property: How to Find It and Deal with Owners

One of the truly immense fortunes to be made awaits the entrepreneur who can assemble the right computer tools to bring together successfully, in anonymity, buyers and sellers of real estate. Imagine, for example, if deeds could be traded with the liquidity of stocks, bonds or other securities. Until that halcyon day, the cumbersome process of seeking out deals, one by one, will remain with us.

Several seminars currently provide information about scouting problem properties. Their advice ranges from studying courthouse deed records for evidence of high–dollar amount financing, foreclosure notices and the like, to finding and contacting owners who appear to be facing financial difficulties.

Once a prospect is located, and the property appears worth considering, the owner must be approached with the utmost diplomacy and tact. Owners in financial trouble often would rather lose everything than be ''gouged by a vulture.'' One recommended negotiating technique is to make clear that in a well-structured deal, everyone wins— the seller walks away with more than he would after fore-closure, the purchaser gets a bargain and the bank resolves a problem loan.

A final recommendation offered by many real estate professionals is to be ready to examine fifty to one hun-dred, or even more, possible deals until you uncover the right one. However, when you do find it, be prepared to move fast.

Repossessed Property: Dealing with Bankers

A strategy that we at VERIBANC have seen investors follow is the development of lists of banks or S&Ls that hold large amounts of foreclosed real estate or as-yet-unforeclosed problem mortgages. Armed with a knowledge of institutions in need of help, investors then approach the bankers with offers to become involved.

The manner in which such an approach is made is ex-ceedingly important. Bankers frequently are not willing to admit to a stranger that they even have "real estate owned" or REO (industry euphemisms for real estate that they would really rather not own). Like most of us, they would rather conduct such sensitive business with people they know and trust. Thus, phone calls to a banker to "tell me about your REO" or gratuitous requests about the bank's policy on financing the purchase of foreclosed properties are likely to be met with polite ignorance or a gentle rebuff. Successful purchases usually involve homework in the form of learning about specific properties held by an institution that needs to get rid of them.

Before the banker is approached, the more successful would-be buyer usually has a good idea of the size of the loan that was defaulted. Forearmed with this knowledge, the buyer can present the banker with a very specific proposal, well tuned to how much the bank has invested in the property.

Banks and S&Ls will often maintain a policy of giving REO over to brokerages. In such cases, it is necessary to convince the banker to consider selling to you before listing it with a broker. If you are a serious buyer with adequate financing, your deal could very well be an attractive alternative to a brokered sale. Remember that by dealing with you, the institution has an immediate hot prospect, and avoids a brokerage commission too.

Be prepared to invest energy in building a relationship with a key officer at the institution that holds REO. Do not be afraid to accept a "no" answer on the first property you seek. However, if you persevere and can enlist the banker's enthusiasm for your investment objectives, you may very well be rewarded with a future bargain. If your rapport is strong enough (and, of course, your financial position too), the bank could end up providing financing for your new REO property.

Selected S&Ls with Foreclosed Property

The list that follows identifies two small savings and loan associations in each state with large amounts of repossessed real estate. Small S&Ls (under $100 million) are more likely to have one or two people, rather than a bureaucracy, to deal with. In developing the list, we required that each S&L possess ''core capital'' in excess of 3 percent of assets, a recent requirement of the federal thrift regulators. This minimizes the chances that, by the time you read this, the institution will have been taken over by the government's Resolution Trust Corporation (and therefore require you to deal with the government). The data is as of year end, 1989. States that are missing, or have only one institution listed, do not have two small S&Ls that meet regulatory capital requirements and hold foreclosed property.

The institutions listed below should be reasonable prospects for real estate deals. Personal business relationships with the appropriate staff should be sought. With sufficient capital to avoid seizure by the regulators, management at these S&Ls should be able to concentrate their attention on improving their asset quality and unloading the real estate they own. Perhaps you can help them and profit in the process.

Selected Small S&L
Associations with REO

State	S&L Name	City
Alabama	Anniston Federal S&L Association	Anniston
Alabama	St. Clair Federal Savings Bank	Pell City
Arkansas	First Federal S&L Association	Camden
Arkansas	First Federal S&L Association	Paragould
California	Equitec Savings Bank	Oakland
California	Amador Valley S&L Association	Pleasanton
Colorado	Gunnison S&L Association	Gunnison
Colorado	Rio Grande S&L Association	Monte Vista
Connecticut	Guardian Federal S&L Association	Bridgeport
Florida	First Federal Savings Bank of De Funiak Springs	De Funiak Springs
Florida	Sovereign Savings Bank	Palm Harbor
Georgia	First Federal Savings Bank	Ashburn
Georgia	Mt. Vernon Federal Savings Bank	Dunwoody
Guam	Guam S&L Association	Agana
Idaho	First Federal S&L Association	Lewiston
Illinois	Security S&L Association	Monmouth
Illinois	First Federal S&L Association of Moline	Moline
Indiana	American Savings, Federal Savings Bank	Munster
Indiana	Fidelity Federal Savings Bank	Marion
Iowa	Grinnell Federal S&L Association	Grinnell
Iowa	Webster City Federal S&L Association	Webster City
Kansas	Argentine S&L Association	Kansas City
Kansas	The Lyons S&L Association	Lyons

State	S&L Name	City
Kentucky	First Federal Savings Bank	Hopkinsville
Kentucky	Family Federal Savings Bank of Paintsville	Paintsville
Louisiana	St. Landry Homestead Federal Savings Bank	Opelousas
Louisiana	Carrollton Homestead Association	New Orleans
Maine	First Federal Savings Bank	Lewiston
Maine	Bethel Savings Bank, Federal Savings Bank	Bethel
Maryland	Potomac Savings Bank, Federal Savings Bank	Silver Spring
Maryland	Golden Prague Bank Loan and Savings Association	Baltimore
Massachusetts	Hyde Park Co-op Bank	Boston
Massachusetts	Colonial Federal Savings Bank	Quincy
Michigan	United Savings Bank, Federal Savings Bank	Farmington Hills
Michigan	New Buffalo Savings Bank, A Federal Savings Bank	New Buffalo
Minnesota	Community Federal S&L Association of Little Falls	Little Falls
Minnesota	Mid-Central Federal Savings Bank	Wadena
Mississippi	Peoples Federal S&L Association	Bay St. Louis
Mississippi	North Central S&L Association	Winona
Missouri	Home S&L Association of Norborne	Norborne
Missouri	The Lexington Bank and Loan Association	Lexington
Montana	American Federal S&L Association of Helena	Helena
Montana	Empire Federal S&L Association	Livingston
Nebraska	Tecumseh Bank and Loan Association	Tecumseh

State	S&L Name	City
Nebraska	Security Federal Savings Bank	Lincoln
Nevada	Atlantic Financial Savings	Las Vegas
New Hampshire	Federal Savings Bank	Dover
New Jersey	Glen Rock S&L Association	Glen Rock
New Jersey	Union City S&L Association	Union City
New Mexico	Charter Bank for Savings, Federal Savings Bank	Santa Fe
New Mexico	Dona Ana S&L Association, Inc.	Las Cruces
New York	Tarrytown and North Tarrytown S&L	Tarrytown
New York	Sunnyside Federal S&L Association of Irvington	Irvington
North Carolina	Davidson Federal S&L Association	Lexington
North Carolina	First Federal S&L Association of Kings Mountain	Kings Mountain
Ohio	Pioneer S&L Company	Marietta
Ohio	First Federal S&L Association	Ironton
Oklahoma	First Federal Savings Bank of Oklahoma	Claremore
Oklahoma	Home Federal S&L Association of Ada	Ada
Oregon	Treasure-Land S&L Association	Ontario
Pennsylvania	Home Savings Association of Pennsylvania	Tamaqua
Pennsylvania	Crusader S&L Association	Rosemont
Puerto Rico	First Tropical Savings Bank, Federal Savings Bank	Santurce
Puerto Rico	Fajardo Federal Savings Bank	Fajardo
Rhode Island	Newport S&L Association	Newport
South Carolina	First South Savings Bank	Columbia
South Carolina	First Trident S&L Corporation	Charleston

State	S&L Name	City
South Dakota	First Federal S&L Association of Beresford	Beresford
South Dakota	American Federal S&L Association of Madison	Madison
Tennessee	Citizens Federal Savings Bank	Rockwood
Tennessee	Lawrenceburg Federal S&L Association	Lawrenceburg
Texas	Balcones Banc Savings Association	San Marcos
Texas	Fayette Savings Association	Lagrange
Utah	Heritage S&L Association	St. George
Utah	First Federal America Bank, A Federal S&L Bank	Logan
Vermont	Springfield S&L Association	Springfield
Vermont	Bennington Co-op S&L Association, Inc.	Bennington
Virginia	Black Diamond S&L Association, Inc.	Norton
Virginia	Bedford Federal Savings Bank	Bedford
Washington	First Federal Savings Bank Northwest	Longview
Washington	Sound S&L Association	Seattle
West Virginia	Doolin Federal S&L Association	New Martinsville
West Virginia	Advance Financial Savings Bank	Wellsburg
Wisconsin	Superior S&L Association	Superior
Wisconsin	Universal Savings Bank Federal Association	Milwaukee
Wyoming	Buffalo Federal S&L Association	Buffalo
Wyoming	Tri-County Federal S&L Association	Torrington

Career Opportunities

Both the banking crisis and technological advances have created a host of professional areas associated with the industry that are well worth considering by anyone looking for a promising future. They include the following:

Bank Officers—Banks small and large need dynamic, creative people who can think up and implement new products, perform project work and communicate well both orally and in writing.

Analysts—Banking and non-banking firms increasingly require personnel with expertise in modeling, statistics and the mathematical tools needed to measure banking institutions in virtually every way imaginable.

Credit Union Administrators—This growing industry needs office people who can work with customers, perform bookkeeping tasks accurately and responsibly and supervise other employees effectively.

Information Officers—Financial institutions of all kinds need computer wizards that can keep data processing equipment operating without trouble, especially for critical tasks that support continuing operations. This is typically a high-pressure, sixty-plus hours per week position, but annual salaries can exceed $100,000.

Regulatory Agents—The federal banking regulatory agencies need analysts, appraisers, collectors, data specialists, examiners, legal practitioners, loan "workout" specialists and a variety of other experienced and entry-level personnel. Since most experts believe the banking crisis will be going on for some time to come, long, secure careers with the FDIC and its sister agencies look promising. The S&L problems, in particular, are likely to be with us well into the year 2000. While the alphabet soup of government agency names that run the S&L bailout (currently including the RTC, its Oversight Board, OTS and Refcorp) may change, the need for people to do the work will not—all of which adds up to promising career potential.

Financial Journalists and TV Reporters—An ever-increasing stream of general information, political events, regulatory activity and technical data about banking institutions must be interpreted for the public and specialized business communities. News publications and the electronic media need articulate people who have, or can develop, a "news sense" and the ability to put together stories. Although banking is too narrow a specialty for most newspeople to devote their attention to exclusively, expertise and awareness in that field is a definite plus for someone seeking top-notch assignments at prestigious news organizations.

CONCLUSION

Most people do not understand the full implications of the rapid changes happening in the banking industry. Recent crises have caused government banking authorities to inject risk into a system that, up until now, has been perceived as risk-free. Stung by the enormous costs of more than a decade of problems, federal banking regulators want the public to help encourage financial institutions to be more conscious of safety. They are demanding that you take responsibility for knowing about and acting upon your bank or thrift's condition. In the words of a former FDIC director James Sexton, ''We do not know how best to convince depositors they should know their banks except to restore the perception that bank depositors actually are at risk.''

To force you to provide this help, federal regulators are purposely increasing the chances that you will suffer if problems develop at your institution. Is your money safe? Increasingly, the answer from the government is ''maybe not.''

APPENDIX

DO YOU HAVE A COMPLAINT ABOUT A BANK, S&L OR CREDIT UNION?

You can contact

- Your bank's management
- Your state banking agency
- Your state's Department of Consumer Affairs
- Your state Attorney General's office

If the institution is

Type of Institution	You Can Complain To
A national bank	The Office of the Comptroller of the Currency Treasury Department of the United States 490 L'Enfant Plaza East, S.W. Washington, DC 20219 Telephone: (202) 287–4265
A Federal Reserve bank	The Federal Reserve System Division of Bank Supervision Washington, DC 20551 Telephone: (202) 452–3236

Type of Institution	You Can Complain To
A state-chartered bank or a savings bank (also, national banks and Federal Reserve banks	The Federal Deposit Insurance Corporation 550 Seventeenth Street, N.W. Washington, DC 20429 Telephone: (800) 424–5488
A privately owned savings and loan association or a federal savings bank	The Office of Thrift Supervision 1700 G Street, N.W. Washington, DC 20429 Telephone: (800) 842–6929 (You will be referred to a district office.)
A government-owned savings and loan association (conservatorship)	The Resolution Trust Corporation 801 Seventeenth Street, N.W. Washington, DC 20429 Telephone: (800) 424–5488
A credit union	The National Credit Union Administration 1776 G Street, N.W. Washington, DC 20456 Telephone: (202) 682–9600 (You will be referred to a regional office.)

VERIBANC CAN HELP YOU
BANK SAFELY

VERIBANC is a bank research firm dedicated to providing people with banking information in easy-to-understand form. The firm has been analyzing banks, S&Ls and credit unions for consumers, business, government and news media clients since 1981.

For a Safety Rating on YOUR BANK — You can find out the rating of any bank, savings and loan association or credit union in the U.S. right now by calling our Instant Rating Service at 1-800-44BANKS, and charging the fee to your Visa or MasterCard. The fee is $10 for one institution and $3 for each additional institution. Or, if you wish, you may simply call the same number and request our free "Know Your Bank" brochure which describes all of our reports on banks and banking safety.

To Help You Find Safe Banks — If you would like to order a current Blue Ribbon Bank Report listing all of the qualifying banks in your region, please send a check with your request to VERIBANC, Inc., P.O. Box 461, Wakefield, MA 01880. The fee for the report is $35. Our gift to you in appreciation for your interest in this book is the $10 discount coupon below which may be used toward the purchase price of the report.

If you have other questions, please do not hesitate to give us a call. We will be more than pleased to help.

- -

Blue Ribbon Bank Report $10.00 Discount Coupon

Name:_____ Phone:_____

City:_____ State:_____ ZIP:_____

Please endorse your check for $25.00   Offer Expires 12/31/90   Duplicates Not Valid